Writing
Like a
Woman

T0355739

POETS ON POETRY · Donald Hall, General Editor

Writing Like a Woman

ALICIA OSTRIKER

Ann Arbor   The University of Michigan Press

1998   1997   1996   9   8   7

Library of Congress Cataloging in Publication Data

Ostriker, Alicia.
  Writing like a woman.

  (Poets on poetry series)
  Includes bibliographical references.
  1. American poetry—Women authors—History and
criticism.   2. American poetry—20th century—History
and criticism.   3. Women poets, American—Biography.
I. Title.   II. Series: Poets on poetry.
PS151.O77   1983   811'.54'099287   82-21959
ISBN 978-0-472-06347-5 (pbk.)

Acknowledgments

Grateful acknowledgment is made to the following journals for permission to reprint previously copyrighted material:

American Poetry Review for "That Story: The Changes of Anne Sexton," *APR* 11, number 4; "May Swenson and the Shapes of Speculation," *APR* 7, number 2; and "Her Cargo: Adrienne Rich and the Common Language," *APR* 8, number 4.

Language and Style for "The Americanization of Sylvia," *Language and Style* 1, number 3 (Summer, 1968).

New Directions for excerpts from the following books by Hilda Doolittle: *Bid Me to Live,* copyright © 1960 by Norman Holmes Pearson; *Collected Poems of H.D.,* copyright © 1925, 1953 by Norman Holmes Pearson; *End to Torment,* copyright © 1979 by New Directions Publishing Corporation; *Helen in Egypt,* copyright © 1961 by Norman Holmes Pearson; *Hermetic Definition,* copyright © 1972 by Norman Holmes Pearson; *Trilogy,* copyright © 1973 by Norman Holmes Pearson. All of the above are reprinted by permission of New Directions Publishing Corporation.

John Schaffner Associates, Inc., agents for the estate of H.D., for passages from *Tribute to Freud* (McGraw-Hill, 1975).

Every attempt has been made to obtain permission to reprint material contained in this volume from copyright holders.

Contents

Introduction
Writing Like a Woman

This book is for those readers who still have no idea why anyone would want to write like a woman, as well as those who know very well why. My wish is to illustrate in these essays a crucial transition, happening in our time, between literary fear and literary courage.

The greatest women writers of the past (at least in the English language, which is the only language I know well enough to survey), with the possible exception of the Brontës, and of Emily more than Charlotte, are always constrained by some pinching corset of timidity, some obscuring veil of inhibition, absent in their male peers. Why did George Eliot punish or kill those heroines who were most restlessly and intelligently like herself? Why does Virginia Woolf explain that she did not write about the experiences of the body because to do so would have incurred censure, where D. H. Lawrence and James Joyce wrote and let censure and censors be damned? Why—this one pains me the most—if there are two poetic geniuses of equal immensity in mid-nineteenth century America, does one of them say "I celebrate myself" and "What I assume you shall assume," while the other one says, "I'm nobody?" Not because the women were more moral or less egotistical than the men, nor because they were obeying their natures, but because they were afraid.

"Tell all the truth but tell it slant," writes Emily Dickinson, not because evasion is intrinsically poetic, but because she is afraid.

The novelist Mary Gordon explains: "I wrote my first novel in the third person. No one would publish it. Then a famous woman writer asked why I had written a first-person novel in the third person. She is a woman of abiding common sense, and so I blushed to tell her: 'I wanted to sound serious. I didn't want to be embarrassing.'"[1]

Adrienne Rich wrote her first explicit work as a woman poet about how the division in "a thinking woman's" life between domestic role and intellectual gifts pushes her toward madness, but she did not have "the courage . . . to use the pronoun 'I'—the woman in the poem is always 'she.'"[2]

In a reading for the BBC, Sylvia Plath describes the poem "Daddy": "Here is a poem spoken by a girl with an Electra complex. Her father died while she thought he was God. Her case is complicated by the fact that her father was also a Nazi and her mother very possibly part Jewish. In the daughter the two strains marry and paralyze each other—she has to act out the awful little allegory once over before she is free of it."[3] But the poem does not say "she," it says "I," and vibrates with a violence that this sanitized synopsis is designed to mask.

Susan Griffin, describing the composition of *Woman and Nature: The Roaring Inside Her,* tells that all the while she wrote the book, "a voice was in me, whispering to me . . . that I had no proof for any of my writing, that I was wildly in error, that the vision I had of the whole work was absurd." The voice was rational, authoritative, male; in fact it was the voice she was attempting in *Woman and Nature* to parody; but it was within her.[4]

The fear governing such quotations is in process of diminishment. In this respect we are changing and can expect to continue changing during our lifetimes, although I must say I have had some young women students whose minds and characters strike me as being more independent than I can ever hope, despite vast deprogramming efforts, to make my own. To tell all the truth and tell it straight has become the program of most women poets. The truth is mysterious enough, and we are ignorant enough of it, so that lives may be well spent in its quest. H.D. at the conclusion of *The Walls Do Not Fall,* the first in her stubbornly innovative trilogy of war poems, writes:

> *we know no rule*
> *of procedure,*
>
> *we are voyagers, discoverers*
> *of the not-known,*
>
> *the unrecorded;*
> *we have no map;*
>
> *possibly we will reach haven,*
> *heaven.*

Rich in "Diving into the Wreck" seeks "the thing itself and not the myth." As the not-known becomes the known and recorded, we may shudder at it. There is the violence of hitherto forbidden emotion, shocking articulations like Plath's "Every woman adores a Fascist," or May Swenson's "Bleeding," or her ironic "Women," which begins:

Women
should be
pedastals
moving
pedastals
moving
to the
motions
of men

Or they
should be
little horses
those wooden
sweet
oldfashioned
painted
rocking
horses

the gladdest things in the toyroom

But there is also the potential for ecstasy and vision, for example in H.D.'s goddesses, or Sexton's sense of the body as an emblem of connectedness enabling her to assert in the poem "In Celebration of My Uterus," when a diagnosis of sickness unto death turns out to be mistaken, that "many women are singing together of this."

"If we have the habit of freedom and the courage to write

exactly as we think," as Woolf puts it in *A Room of One's Own*, writing like a woman simply means writing like what one actually is, in sickness and health, richer or poorer, belly and bowels, the consonants and the vowels too. We may have a general sense that women poets are more likely than men, at the present time, to write in detail about their bodies, to take power relationships as a theme, to want to speak with a strong rather than a subdued voice; are less likely to seek distance, more likely to seek intimacy, in poetic tone. But generalization would be foolish here. "Woman poet," like "American poet" or "French poet" or "Russian poet," allows—even insists on—diversity, while implying something valuable in common, some shared language and life, of tremendous importance to the poet and the poet's readers.

I began reading poetry by women intensively in the summer of 1976. I had recently completed the task of writing annotations for an edition of the complete poems of William Blake, an endeavor that swallowed several years of my working life but was also greatly illuminating. Next to Blake, almost anything looked pale. But the body of poetry by women in our time constituted work that was as unorthodox, as path-breaking and rule-breaking, and in many ways as exciting and as difficult for me to read as Blake's. Everywhere I read in women's poems I found passages that touched my personal identity, experience and ideas, in places no poetry had touched before. It was not always gratifying. Where the poems confirmed my feelings they sometimes drove me into pits of despair and anger from which I had great difficulty extracting myself. Where I disagreed with a woman poet's ideology I was furious with her in a way that I would never be with a man, as if she were telling lies about me in front of the television cameras. Trudging through the middle of my journey as I was, when the poets said, "You must change your life, you must change your art," I resisted. The poems won, after all, because they were throwing a rope down a well. Somebody seized the rope and held on.

The five poets I have written of here are brave women and strong writers, from whom I have learned and with whom I have wrestled. Each of these essays came about, in fact, because I was tugged and pulled by some particular poet, seduced and irritated, and needed to write to clarify my perplexity. They are very different from each other. Only one was, like Blake, a visionary, as well as a student of mythology and the occult. Only one has become a feminist activist. Nature is a primary subject of one. Two took their own lives—a matter not to be ignored—but the first seems to have been dominated by anger and self-hatred from the beginning, while the second fought hard with love, greed and laughter to save herself, and failed.

I have tried to understand what is unique in each writer: the sources of her power, her style, her playfulness, her wit, grace, coarseness, intellectuality, the themes she chooses to address. I have tried to suggest the pain and fear confronted by each, the risks taken, the phases of her development. This last point is important because only in our own time do we see many women poets having careers in the same sense that men always have, which involves solving problems and moving on to other problems. *A Change of World* was the prophetic title of Adrienne Rich's first volume. A later one of her books is called *The Will to Change*. It is a joy, reading through a woman's work, to watch her grow too large for herself, shed her skin and emerge new.

My two concluding essays began as talks at forums exploring, respectively, the subjects of "gender and creativity" and "women and myth." In the latter it was my good fortune to sit on a panel with Sandra Gilbert and Rachel DuPlessis, poet-critics whose work parallels, stimulates and challenges my own. In exploring the genesis of work I have written, I necessarily include theirs.

A book such as this leaves unanswered a battery of fascinating questions. Do women write differently about nature from men? What kind of God do women need? What does love—of herself, of men, of other women—mean to a woman, and how about hate? Does the marginal position of the woman poet generate a different way of thinking about politics or history, or even language itself? I have not at all attempted in these essays to describe the *chorale* of women poets in America. Here are a few of the voices "singing together of this." Hundreds of others exist, and they form a regional and racial mix that the present essays do not begin to suggest. It is self-evident to me that a literary history which selects only a few writers to represent a period is as partial as the old sort of history of nations which chronicled only kings and battles and not the lives of the people ruled and fought over—whose movements are in some ways the true movements of history. I believe that the flood of writing by eloquent women in our own time will alter the mainstream of American poetry. To explore and chart the breadth, depth and power of these waters will be the work of another book.

NOTES

1. Mary Gordon, "The Parable of the Cave, or: in Praise of Watercolors," in *The Writer on Her Work: Contemporary Women Writers Reflect on their Art and Situation,* edited by Janet Sternburg (New York: W. W. Norton & Co., 1980), p. 30.
2. Adrienne Rich, "When We Dead Awaken: Writing as Re-vision," in her *On Lies, Secrets and Silence: Selected Prose 1966–1978,* pp. 44–45.
3. Ted Hughes, ed., *Collected Poems of Sylvia Plath* (New York: Harper & Row, 1981), p. 293.
4. Susan Griffin, "Thought on Writing: A Diary" in *The Writer on Her Work: Contemporary Women Writers Reflect on their Art and Situation,* edited by Janet Sternburg (New York: W. W. Norton & Co., 1980), p. 112.

The Poet as Heroine
Learning to Read H.D.

Those who recall the name recall mostly that she was discovered by Ezra Pound and was "the perfect *imagiste.*" For a while, in the twenties and early thirties, she wrote exquisitely "frozen" and "crystalline" lyrics in free verse, mostly on classic Greek themes, and then she disappeared from view. Those who have read Hugh Kenner's *The Pound Era* may remember that she was quasi engaged to Pound in their Pennsylvanian youth before they both became figures in the London literary scene, that she had a brief marriage with Richard Aldington, that she had bisexual affairs, that she was psychoanalyzed by Freud, and that in Kenner's opinion "Imagism" must be understood as a not very significant pebble in the Poundian stream.

But I find that to read H.D. I must forget whatever I have learned about Imagism. It doesn't fit. Even her earliest poems have a power that reduces the tidy and tiny Imagism box to splinters. I find too, as others have lately been finding, that the lyric verse H.D. is best known for was succeeded by something altogether different: a set of long poems written during and after World War II, and until the poet's death in 1961. These are works that wrestle with the great modernist issues of faith's collapse and the possibility of reconstruction; self and society; the nature of language and the value of poetry in history; the meaning of the imagination. And they are works in an ancient genre, the quest, but with a significant difference. Instead of a poet-hero, these long, arduous, glorious poems center themselves on a poet-heroine. And that, as Robert Frost might have said, makes all the difference.

I want to begin this essay by sketching, very briefly, what seems to me H.D.'s position as a visionary. Then I want to look at the three main phases of her poetry: the mostly pre–World War I verse of *Sea Garden* (1916), the middle period which includes the volumes *Hymen* (1921), *Heliodora* (1924) and *Hippolytus Temporizes* (1927), and finally the late work on which her reputation as a major modern poet will ultimately rest—the war poems collected under the title *Trilogy* (1944–46), the revisionist myth of *Helen in Egypt* (1960), and the posthumously published *Hermetic Definition* (1972).[1]

The story will be punctuated, early on, by disaster, but will conclude in recovery. The Great War inflicted on H.D. the great wounds of her lifetime, and her poetry at first could not deal with war directly. Then, after long silence, it could and did, with remarkable results. H.D. by the end of her career became not only the most gifted woman poet of our century, but one of the most original poets—the more I read her the more I think this—in our language. I hope I can convey my wonder, however belated, in discovering her.

I.

First of all, H.D. is a visionary poet. By this I mean that she is one of a tiny group of poets for whom, behind the flux of secular existence, there exist permanent sacred realities that are both supremely beautiful and supremely forceful. The poet apprehends these realities, personally and intimately, during states of altered consciousness: "vision," "trance," "dream." Plato said a poet in such a state was being inspired by the gods, and was mad. Today we use, instead of the dangerous term inspiration, the comfortable term "imagination," about which people can say, "Oh, it's only your imagination." As if what is imagined were not real. But it is real. It is also difficult to seize, which is why Shelley calls the poet's excited mind "a fading coal."

As William James tells us in *The Varieties of Religious Experience*, rather little is dogmatic about sacred experiences, and almost nothing is prescriptively moral—until, of course, the experience is interpreted. Visions are simply so true to the visionary, and so splendid, that the visionary may feel prepared to sacrifice anything for them. The dreamer's rapture is like love or drunkenness, an addiction of the whole being. Within history the trajectory of vision is that it lapses into doctrine, and doctrine solidifies into institution, so that the seer who personally communicates with an unpredictable divinity is in time replaced by a priest whose god hops in a gilded vessel and follows regulations. "Thus men forget," says Blake, "that all deities reside in the human breast."

The visionary poet's alternative is to shape sacred experience into poems, not doctrine, and to retrieve from the world's thickets of orthodoxy, age-old and age-thick, the sharp berries of heterodox truth. To the visionary poet, poetry is not primarily Literature. It must be beautiful and forceful in order to bear witness and tribute to its source. Then these attributes, beauty and force, are borrowed by secular literature, like a child wearing its parents' clothes.

To read H.D., early and late work, is like reading early and late Blake. I think she also resembles Edmund Spenser, and the John Milton of the devil's party. Among her contemporaries, we must obviously pair her with Pound—who was her discoverer, her earliest lover-cohort, her alter ego in a way, maybe her animus, the poet against whom she was still obsessively measuring herself even at the very end of her life. She is also like Williams. There is a rough pattern to some of these careers, and here is a rough oversimplification of it. Early work is experimental, even revolutionary, and yet formally excellent. The poet writes lyric poems, vigorous, buoyant, highly idealistic and deceptively simple. The sound of them is exquisite chamber music. The poems celebrate an imagined world. They also demonstrate, but do not laboriously analyze, the poet's contempt for society as it is and for the usual structures of personality as they are. So we have aesthetic brilliance coupled with ideological originality.

Then comes catastrophe. For Milton it was the ignominious collapse of Cromwell's English Commonwealth, to which the poet had given his eyes. For Blake: the failure of the French Revolution, which he had expected to bring about the end of human tyranny and repression: and his own reduction to abject poverty. For Pound: World War I, the death of Gaudier-Brzeska, the hideous (to him) triumph of bourgeois values in England and America. In all these cases, public neglect, ridicule or ostracism provides ample evidence that what the poet has lived for has failed completely. Depending on where in the poet's life the shock strikes, there may or may not be a period of post-trauma transitional works. Ultimately there emerges the poem "including history," which will engage the rest of the poet's life, and deal with time, loss and reconstruction. The goal is wholeness, to be won from fragmentation. What is to be repaired is at once self and not-self, a shattered self-doubting mind and a faithless world. One means to this end is strenuous introspection. Another is the reexamination of mythic sources, polycultural and polytemporal, leading to the shaping of a new myth. At first, formulas like "make it new" or "I gather the limbs of Osiris" have a fine ring. Later the lifework becomes, very plainly, an agonizing struggle.

I want to emphasize the dimension of struggle. I think we can assume that the youthful visionary artist, flush with arrogant clarity, believes (irrationally) that the publication of poems will magically change the world. When the world not only fails to change but becomes more brutal and stupid than the poet had imagined possible, when allies defect, when the bitter fact is digested that "beauty is hated" even after one has made one's excellent early poems, there comes a grinding shifting of gears. The poet starts over, no longer on the wings of confident enthusiasm, but instead with a stubbornness "not to be changed by space or time," as Milton's Satan says. "I must create a system or be enslaved by another man's. I will not reason or compare. My business is to create," says Blake. "Rigor of beauty is the quest. But how will you find beauty, when it is locked in the mind past all remonstrance?" asks Williams. Pound "tried to make a paradiso / terrestre." And

H.D., accused by critics of escapism, comparing herself in post–World War II London with a flight of legendary birds circling above the drowned Atlantis, writes, "So I would rather drown, remembering":

> I would rather beat in the wind, crying to these others:
>
> Yours is the more foolish circling,
> yours is the senseless wheeling
>
> round and round—yours has no reason—
> I am seeking heaven;
>
> yours has no vision,
> I see what is beneath me, what is above me,
>
> what men say is-not—I remember,
> I remember, I remember—
>
> Trilogy, p. 121

What H.D. says she seeks is sometimes called "The Hesperides," sometimes "Paradise," and the memories from which she tries to reconstruct in her late poems "all myth, the one reality" include Egyptian, Hebrew, Greek and Christian myths, occult lore, alchemy. Like her brethren, she is eclectic and heterodox, not by accident. Reality begins in the human imagination, and must pass through it again to be resurrected alive. How else, besides, is it to be proved that all orthodoxy is in itself false, that only what the imagination seizes as truth is true?

II.

Sea Garden, published when the poet was thirty, is H.D.'s *Songs of Innocence.* Blake's *Songs* were published when he was thirty-two. Or it is her Spenserian eclogues, or her "L'Allegro" and "Il Penseroso." Young poets classically cut their teeth on pastoral poetry, and H.D. is knowingly or unknowingly doing the same thing as many of her forebears, defining ideal self through ideal landscape. But it is an unusually wild, unwomblike landscape. A harsh climate shapes the beauty of the "sea rose," "sea lily" and other wind- and salt-beaten flowers the poet admires:

> You are clear,
> O rose, cut in rock,
> hard as the descent of hail.

She likes dangerous cliff-vistas, seascapes, high inaccessible temples and their gods, and solitude. She has a lust for nature's indifferent purity, illustrated by moments of violence that illuminate perception as lightning illuminates landscape. There are chains of active verbs: cut and break, catch and drive, shudder, stagger, dare, strike. This is very like Robinson Jeffers on Big Sur—did Jeffers read H.D.?—except that his verse resembles chunks of coal mined from earth. Hers resembles diamond, a further degree of compression. There is also, throughout, the theme of pursuit. In "Sea-Gods," "they say there is no hope/to conjure you," but the poet and her ilk persist:

> You will thunder along the cliff—
> break—retreat—get fresh strength—
> gather and pour weight upon the beach . . .
>
> You will bring myrrh-bark
> and drift laurel-wood from hot coasts!
> When you hurl high—high—
> we will answer with a shout.

A reader need not know that "myrrh" (one of the exotic gifts in the Christian nativity story, which H.D. would use decades later in *The Flowering of the Rod* as a figure for the Magdalen's gift of self to god, and the poet's gift of her poetry) is a plant with a phallic flower, or that "laurel" is Apollo's plant, sacred to poets, to sense that the poem is running on adrenalin, or to be bent with its longing: "you will come,/you will answer our taut hearts,/you will break the lie of men's thought,/and cherish and shelter us." Permanence of land, flux of water and wind, clean descriptions of shorelines, borderlines, interfaces of all sorts, physical and mental, the mysterious excitement of places where opposed elements meet: these are H.D.'s key images, along with the thirst to unite opposites, especially sexual opposites. To "break the lie" is a male deed, to "cherish and shelter" a female one.

One implication of the theme of fearlessness and the anti-inland, antisocietal, antisafety elation of *Sea Garden* is that inland life is corrupt and tame. The wild natural settings enable the poet to imagine an existence unconfined by the genteel feminine proprieties that governed her Philadelphia girlhood. She can defy her astronomer-father's rationality and her mother's middle-class conventionality. More important: the asocial settings make possible a book that is intensely erotic yet without sexual polarization. *Sea Garden's* many flower images, for example, effectively redefine one of our culture's oldest emblems of feminine virginity and the frailty of feminine beauty, by being strong, not weak, rather like O'Keeffe's flowers in a comparably stark environment, though without the painter's enlargement of scale. The poet's persona is often androgynous; when it is male, as with the sailors of "The Helmsman," "Sea Gods" and "The Shrine," it adores and submits; when female, as in "Huntress," it is equipped with spears. As with her many images of plant-surrounded pursuit and penetration, the poet can be both an enveloping "heat" and the wind that must "rend open the heat, / cut apart the heat, / rend it to tatters." There are only three love poems in the volume, none heterosexual.

What gives these poems their excitement, quite apart from their crisp "imagistic" purity and their lack of what Pound called "emotional slither" is, I think, their encoding of active desire. Desire: a property of the self. The poet's need for wildness is a need for her own wildness. Her courting of death is a courting of liberty. The desire for union with beloved cold and virginal yet erotic deities foreshadows the wish to "close the gap in consciousness" that H.D. in *Tribute to Freud* associates with emotional division from her mother, anticipating the insistence in many women's poems today that to recover one's mother-child link is to become a complete being. "A woman *is* her mother. That's the main thing," says Anne Sexton. In much of H.D.'s late work, a woman *is* her mother-goddess. Part of the point is that "the lie of men's thought" claims we cannot be united with what's sacred—nature, our parents, the past, our own potential passionate completeness—and the poet says we can.

That H.D.'s settings at this point are "Greek" seems to me relatively accidental. In fact, she explained to Norman Holmes Pearson late in life that she got these settings from the Maine and Rhode Island seashores she visited in childhood. The scenes are made "Greek" but left generalized to stress that the poet describes an imaginary landscape, or better yet, a landscape *of* the imagination, a map of the poet's mind. At this stage the mind is clear, proud, wild, dedicated to its own integrity, and submissive to nothing but the laws of nature and art. The Great War, in every way, would break that pride, humiliate that integrity, undermine the poet's faith in herself, confuse her clarity, force her to confront sexual and other dualisms she would rather have denied, and set her to the long labor of reintegration.

III.

War and sex, sex and war, inseparable. H.D. seems to have sought, over and over, a man whose love for her would be indistinguishable from his love for beauty and truth. What she found, too often for it to be accidental, was something more predictable.

I say she found it. But nothing in the world is so simple. I mean, really, she bought into it. Or do I? Pound of course was the first of H.D.'s failed romances. The Pound-figure in her 1927 novel *Her* "wanted Her, but he wanted a Her he called decorative." He quotes to her the line, "You are a poem though your poem's naught." She resists him, prefers another woman, loses both—they betray her with each other—and at the novel's end she is recovering from a breakdown. Thirty years later in her memoir *End to Torment*, as Pound is emerging from St. Elizabeth's, her attitude toward him as a writer is adoring, and she is filled with electric sexual memories. At the same time he is depicted as a sexual bully, a collector and discarder of female acolytes; had their engagement not been broken and Dorothy Shakespeare's fate been hers, she muses, "Ezra would have destroyed me and the center . . . of my poetry." Here is her recollection of the moment in the British Museum tea room when Ezra took from Hilda Doolittle the poem which would initiate her publishing career:

> "But Dryad . . . this is poetry." He slashed with a pencil. "Cut this out, shorten this line. 'Hermes of the Ways' is a good title. I'll send this to Harriet Monroe of *Poetry*. Have you a copy? Yes? Then we can send this, or I'll type it when I get back. Will this do?" And he scrawled "H.D. Imagiste" at the bottom of the page. (*End to Torment*, p. 18)

This is not far from girlish locker-room boasting. He said he *loved* me, girls have whispered to each other for centuries. Then consider the nuances: the "slashing" of her poem, the signing of her name for her.

He defines her. By the same token he can destroy her. He, not she, is strong, authoritative. "He" is any man she is attracted to, physically, emotionally, intellectually.

The scene in the tea room took place in October 1912. H.D. a year later married the idealistic fellow-poet and fellow-imagist, Richard Aldington. The War began the following year. In 1916 Aldington enlisted in the British Army, and H.D. took over his position as assistant editor of *The Egoist*. She had had a miscarriage which left her frail and possibly frigid. Aldington soon commenced an affair with the less intellectual and high-strung, more earthy American woman in the flat upstairs. The Aldingtons separated, although there was no legal divorce until 1938. In 1918 H.D.'s brother was killed in France. Her father suffered a stroke on hearing the news and died shortly after.

Until a definitive biography appears, we will not know how

the poet reacted to the losses of a child, a husband, a brother, a father. But in the fictions H.D. wrote about this period in her life, she portrays the poet-heroine as a being who is excruciatingly passive, who depends on men to share her faith in "worlds of past beauty that were future beauty" and to cooperate in creating moments of mystic "bliss." When they fail her she does not fight, is not angry, is merely paralyzed. In *Bid Me to Live* the heroine is manipulated and rejected first by her warcoarsened husband, then by "Rico" (D. H. Lawrence), who has promised erotic and spiritual companionship. Criticizing a poem she sends him, Rico snappishly writes: "I don't like the second half of the Orpheus sequence as well as the first. Stick to the woman speaking. How can you know what Orpheus feels? It's your part to be woman, the woman vibration, Euridice should be enough." Her response, "But if he could enter, so diabolically, into the feelings of women, why should she not enter into the feelings of men?" remains unspoken and unshared. She imagines a way to escape "the biological catch" of sex roles: if two artists pair, "then the danger met the danger, the woman was man-woman, the man was woman-man." The men in the novel think otherwise. Shortly after invoking her ideal of androgynous mutuality between artist-lovers, the novelist repeats one of the novel's refrains: "The war will never be over."

War in H.D.'s fiction is unglamorously and absolutely destructive, "an actuality, holocaust . . . it was annihilation itself that gaped at her . . . the past had been blasted to hell, you might say . . . was being bombed to bits, was no more." "Holocaust" is the largest possible image of all betrayals and obliterations, and the immediate cause of the small ones, Her child's death coincides with the death of England's youth. Both are intolerable to her. It is also war that comes between her and her husband, making his infidelity inevitable, for she attempts to remind him of his commitment to art when he does not wish to be reminded, but only to be admired and comforted:

> Beauty is truth, truth beauty. But could this truth [the war] be
> beautiful? Maybe it was. They had shouted of honour and sacri-

fice for two years, three years now . . . seasons revolved around horrors until one was numb . . . they were past feeling anything; she was. He was right, then, maybe, when he said, "You don't feel anything."

The refrain "the war will never be over" has several linked meanings. Its obsessive repetition within the novel stands not only for the heroine's inability to see to the end of a present conflict, but her terror that the past, too, will have been irrevocably cancelled—and not primarily a personal past, but Europe's visible and invisible heritage of human encounters with beauty. In *Murex* the heroine's drunken husband tells her, "There ain't going to be any more poets." In *Bid Me to Live* she wonders desperately if architectural monuments can possibly "remain even after they were bombed to hell, one way or another, a pattern in the air?" "The war will never be over" is also the sexual war, the war between men and women, which will never be over as long as there is sexual polarization instead of H.D.'s relation of "man-woman" and "woman-man." Yet another meaning is female rivalry, the division of the female image into a cerebral-emotional woman whom the soldier-husband loves spiritually and a physical-seductress woman whom he wants sexually because she makes him forget his fear of death and his numbed aesthetic sensitivity. Finally and most radically there is the war within the poet's self, between faith in her convictions and despairing self-doubt.

Sex and war, war and sex, sex and war and the loss of her true self and true vision: it was precisely this that the idealization of solitude in *Sea Garden* was, one thinks in retrospect, designed to protect herself against. At this point the evident stubbornness of H.D.'s character becomes crucial. Everything she writes after World War I reacts to the trauma of division and self-division, and expresses in one fashion or another the will to heal, to make whole through the power of imagination what has been broken in her life and the life of Europe. For the remainder of her career she works in response to two handicaps, transforming both into the substance of her art. One is the handicap of the visionary in an environment hostile to vision. The other is that of a woman writing in a world which is politically, socially, intellectually dominated by men, some of whom she loves, some of whom betray her—and who insists on reimagining her relationship to the world and to the men in it. "Resurrection is a sense of direction," she was to write in *The Flowering of the Rod.* Bit by bit she was to resurrect herself, although not until her final years does she arrive at the unity she required.

IV.

If *Sea Garden* represents Innocence, the postwar poetry represents Experience. Technically the form remains the same: exquisitely lyric free verse, gemlike, perfect. But the imagery changes, becoming less white, chaste and sculptural, richer, more deliquescent and glowing, more full of fire, darkness, gold, deep reds and purples, spilled wine. Rather than the cool deities of *Sea Garden,* there appear figures whose worship signifies surrender to the flesh, passion, procreation: Bacchus, Hymen, Demeter, Circe, Aphrodite. Instead of integrity and androgyny we have "love and love sweetness," we have the image of lovers as swords, we have lines like "her strength was twisted for his bearing," conflating rape and childbirth. We have the question "Could Eros be kept? . . . Is it bitter to give back / love to your lover / if he crave it? . . . or is it sweet?" and the cry that "to sing love, love must first shatter us."

Throughout her middle period, most of H.D.'s poetry—translations as well as original poems—can be seen as an attempt to come to terms with the experience of art and love betrayed; and here begins her discovery of what "Greece" could do for a poet besides provide wild settings, generalized nature-gods, and models of poetic craftsmanship. "Greece" meant a set of specific myths that were eternally true because they were eternally beautiful. To recreate these myths was to unite a spiritual obligation with a private need. Art would triumphantly restore what war had appeared to destroy, and at the same time the artist would understand and validate her life by discovering where her experience and mythic patterns—an individual modern psyche and a collective ancient one—coalesced.

The largeness of the step she took at this point requires special notice. Pound, promoting the idea of making classicism new by basing it in individual psychology, had written in 1912:

> I believe that Greek myth arose when someone having passed through delightful psychic experience tried to communicate it to others and found it necessary to screen himself from persecution. . . . Speaking esthetically, the myths are explanations of mood; you may stop there, or you may probe deeper . . . I know, I mean, one man who understands Persephone and Demeter, and one who understands the Laurel, and another who has, I should say, met Artemis. These things are for them *real*.

In 1918, in Pound's charming "Religio, or, the Child's Guide to Knowledge":

> What is a god?
> A god is an eternal state of mind . . .
> When is a god manifest?
> When the states of mind take form.
> When does a man become a god?
> When he enters into one of these states of mind.[2]

So far so good, and it goes without saying that "man" understands, enters into, etc. Then Pound embarked upon the *Cantos* and became the Odysseus-Dante redivivus whose goal was "the 'magic moment' or moment of metamorphosis, bust through from quotidian into 'divine or permanent world.'"

But the new event in H.D.'s middle period (whether this constitutes deliberate upstaging of Pound as well as divergence from him I cannot say) is that the distinction between what is personally quotidian and what is suprapersonally divine collapses. There is no need to "bust through"—and should we observe, by the way, the sexual implication of Pound's metaphor? The poems are there already; the poet herself assumes the personae of gods and goddesses, heroes and heroines, who psychically absorb her, so that they seethe with a private life which is both hers and theirs. This is not to say that the artist occupies, for H.D., a peaceful or privileged position. Art is an absolute value, but it is intimately associated with conflict. The conflict may be pleasant, as in the title poem of *Heliodora*, where two poets drink all night inventing epithets for a beautiful mistress. More typically, H.D.'s Pygmalion is burned alive for his blasphemous confusion of the gods with his sculptures of them. Cassandra's gift of prophecy is a curse. Lynceus the superhumanly far-sighted is hated by the Argonauts whose ship he guides and is tormented by monsters he alone perceives under the water's surface. Still less can we say that Love, also an absolute value in H.D.'s mythic world, is other than absolutely problematic for those who feel it.

Following the dissolution of her marriage, H.D.'s first book was called *Hymen*, a title invoking female anatomy, a male god, and an act of rapture that is also an act of rupture. Its title piece, a pageant structured like an elaborate tumescence-detumescence, appears at first reading to be the most prettily ritualized celebration of feminine sexuality since Edmund Spenser's "Epithalamion." The bride, a silent "veiled symbolic figure," receives erotically emblematic flower offerings from processions of girls who are at once her bridal "society" and a projection of the youthful part of her life cycle. The flamboyant scarlet-garbed "Love" who enters after them may be either Eros or an individual bridegroom—or he may be the personification of a maiden's fantasy, an aspect of her own imagination. "Love" sings the masque's one solo, employing a bee-flower metaphor unlike anything in H.D.'s earlier work, though it recalls a half-dozen Emily Dickinson poems, with its warm gold-flecked bee who "seeks with honey-thighs to sway / And drink the very flower away":

> Quivering he sways and quivering clings
> (Ah, rare her shoulders drawing back!)
> One moment, then the plunderer slips
> Between the purple flower-lips.

If we read "Hymen" as a response to H.D.'s destroyed marriage, it seems a generous tribute to vanished joy, and a gesture in the direction of defining the poet as poet-priestess, composer of sacred rituals. Only as a sort of aftertaste may we sense. what Yeats called a counter-truth: that a polarized active-passive, plunderer-prey pattern in sexuality makes the "object" of love faceless, voiceless, blank.

Of the poems which develop, fiercely and subversively, the counter-truth, the simplest are those which implicitly or explicitly indict male "arrogance and ruthlessness," male fickleness, the godlike male capacity to captivate and betray a woman.

Some of H.D.'s portraits of abandoned poets, heroines and goddesses are laments touched with hope. Some stand coldly beyond hope. "Euridice" anticipates by fifty years the discovery by other women poets that the story of Orpheus can be told from a feminine perspective. In H.D.'s version of the lost bride's monologue, a woman loved by a great poet is better off among the terrors of hell than by his side. "Helen," shocking in its brevity, tells us that woman-as-erotic-object is hated by those who pretend to love her, and that the only good beauty is a dead beauty who can be embalmed in art:

> All Greece hates
> the still eyes in the white face . . .

One thinks again of the passivity of Marlowe's "face that launched a thousand ships"; of Poe's adolescent-fantasy "Helen" and his conviction that the death of a beautiful woman is the most poetic subject possible; of Yeats' irritated portrait of Maud Gonne in "No Second Troy." In "Callypso Speaks," taken from the opening episode of *The Odyssey*, H.D. renders the classic pattern of male mobility and female immobility as a bitterly comic double monologue. The deserted Callypso curses Odysseus' stupidity and calls all nature to witness that "man is clumsy and evil," while Odysseus sails cheerfully homeward recounting to himself the useful gifts Callypso has given him, including "peace in her cave":

Odysseus (on the sea)
     she gave me a wooden flute
     and a mantle,
     she wove me this wool
Callypso (from land)
     for man is a brute and a fool.

These are poems of white-heat irony, and no ironic woman poet since has improved on them. They are the finished product, the blade that slices without effort. One might consider, alongside these pieces, H.D.'s translations of passages from Euripides' *Iphigenia,* the drama of a girl slaughtered by warriors, and his *Bacchae,* in which a man who refuses to worship Dionysus is slaughtered by his own mother. Depiction of brutality, fantasy of punishment—like the originals, the translations are merciless. They are also, for H.D., a spiritual dead end. Closer to her struggle for a psychic pattern that would transcend rather than perpetuate the wars of the sexes are the "Hippolytus" poems in *Hymen* and the ironic-tragic drama modelled on Euripides, *Hippolytus Temporizes.*

It is clear that what drew H.D. to Euripides' *Hippolytus* was the triangular situation of a sensitive hero torn between opposed female principles. On one side there is Hippolyta-Artemis, wild and virginal, with whom the poet identifies. On the other side there is Phaedra-Aphrodite, sophisticated and voluptuous, the rival. Euripides' Phaedra, when the chaste Hippolytus scornfully rejects her lust, accuses him of rape and thus precipitates the tragedy. But H.D.'s Phaedra, like "Bella" in the London flat upstairs, successfully seduces him. And what is remarkable about H.D.'s revision of Euripides' plot is not simply that she makes it fit her personal story, but that she makes it fit her need to imagine what it means to be the Other, the Enemy, to dissolve enmity by perceiving that what opposes the self is already latent within the self. Since she renders each of the main characters—cold Artemis, threatened by the encroachment of human cities, torrid Phaedra writhing with desire, innocent and self-deluding Hippolytus—with equal empathy, we are made to sympathize both with the young man's slide from worship of a chaste goddess to love of a sensual woman, and with the woman's painful and self-destructive desire. Psychologically, H.D.'s most touching stroke is to make the desperate Phaedra seduce her prey by impersonating the chaste Artemis, a device quite worthy of Euripides.

If *Hippolytus Temporizes* dramatizes the defeat of H.D.'s virginal and isolated early self by Aphrodite, it is a defeat in which the poet acquiesces. *Heliodora* includes a sequence of painfully self-revealing lyrics dedicated to the "shameless and radiant" goddess of love. Here H.D. claims, defying charges of coldness and cowardice in love, that she has offered Aphrodite "the love of my lover / for his mistress." Though it is understood that worship of "the bright goddess" destroyed Troy and breaks individuals, the poet endorses those devotees who are most arrogant in her praise:

> I Nossis stand by this:
> I state that love is sweet:
> if you think otherwise
> assert what beauty
> or what charm
> after the charm of love
> retains its grace?
>
> "Honey" you say:
> Honey? I say "I spit
> honey out of my mouth . . ."

And for herself H.D. boasts in a startlingly intimate image:

> though I break,
> crushed under the goddess' hate,
> though I fall beaten at last,
> so high have I thrust my gaze
> up into her presence.

These are not, it should be noticed, poems commending lovers. They are poems worshipping Love herself, and demonstrating the artist's capacity for self-surrender.

Two female figures in H.D.'s postwar period escape romantic thralldom[3] and point forward to her later work. H.D.'s "Demeter" is a rather realistic mother who resents men's rituals and the thick sculptures they make for her to inhabit. She claims that she (not Zeus, the brutal begetter) is the savior of the infant Dionysus. Her terms, like Adrienne Rich's insistence on "the thing itself and not the myth" fifty years later in "Diving into the Wreck," assert the primacy of female experience against traditions that purport to explain it:

> enough of tale, myth, mystery, precedent—
> a child lay on the earth asleep.

This Demeter also reveals an unexpected dimension in the tale of Persephone's rape, beyond the characterization of masculine lust as violent:

> What of her—
>
> mistress of Death—
> what of his kiss?
>
> Ah strong were his arms to wrest
> slight limbs from the beautiful earth . . .
> Ah, strong were the arms that took
> (ah, evil the heart and graceless)
> but the kiss was less passionate!

If in this poem H.D. hints that the ultimately "passionate" eroticism is between mother and daughter, "Thetis" hints that it is between mother and son. Here the sea-goddess mother of Achilles rises "alert, all blue and wet" to the beach where his heroic sandal has imprinted the sand, and with unmistakeable seductiveness "lay along the burning sand / a river's blue." Both poems imply that the dangerous figure of the passionate god-hero-warrior becomes emotionally safer if he is transformed to a mother's son. The figure of a divine mother who absorbs some of Artemis' inviolability, some of Aphrodite's sensuousness, is one to which H.D. returns again and again in her late work, using her more and more explicitly as a counterforce to the violent power of masculinity. In *Tribute to the Angels* she will be the Lady who appears to the war-torn poet and endorses her as scribe, and in *The Flowering of the Rod* she is the two Marys, Virgin and Magdalen. In *Helen in Egypt* she will be Isis-Thetis, the heroine's spiritual mother and sensual self, responsible for transforming Achilles' will to conquest into capacity for love. In *Winter Love* she will be the midwife who cruelly and kindly brings the dying poet the *Espérance*—the poem of hope—she has just borne, after desertion by that lover she calls Odysseus, who is still Ezra Pound.

Meanwhile, to define the precise direction of H.D.'s postwar poetry the best parallel remains Pound. Both writers continued to believe that ancient myth embodied permanently pertinent actualities, that the modern world disjoined from its past was crippled, and that the artist's task was to rejoin what was sundered. But Pound, after renouncing his early aestheticism in "Mauberley," centers the *Cantos* increasingly on the civic rather than the private virtue of art; ballasts myth with history, economics, philosophy, and a set of mentally and physically virile heroes; and defines the artist as public pedagogue instead of private individual. H.D. plunges into myth increasingly for its psychological resonance; centers her work on private and inner, not public and outer, conflict; struggles to define meanings for femininity in a world of male power, while undermining the stature of traditional heroes as seen from a feminine perspective. For her the artist is marked and burdened by Love, a "state of mind" from which Pound, notwithstanding Aphrodite's glamorous walk-ons in the *Cantos,* is increasingly distant.

In a sense H.D. in her middle years solves the problem of the dissociated modern sensibility more fully than any writer of her time. In another sense her strategy is evasive. Her personal fusion of past and present is so smooth that she need not deal with time and history. She avoids calling attention to the fact that her versions of myth are strongly revisionist. Concentrating on Love and Art—acceptably feminine themes— she protects herself from direct encounter with certain traditionally masculine issues, in particular the issue of war. I would connect this evasion—this incapacity—with the fact that her postwar poetry remains full of unredeemed divisions, its strongest poems structured around sexual polarities; that the overall tone of this work, however splendidly accomplished, is painful; and that her poetic creativity declined and almost halted in the early 1930s.

V.

A *Collected Poems* composed of H.D.'s first three volumes appeared in 1925. Two novels and two more books of poems followed in the next half dozen years and were received with less enthusiasm than her early work. She was by this time living, mostly in Switzerland, with the historical novelist Winifred Ellerman (known as Bryher) who had fallen in love first with H.D.'s poems, then with the poet. Bryher had seen H.D. through severe illness and the birth of her daughter Perdita in 1919, when both mother and infant were expected to die. In 1920, after the poet's nervous collapse, Bryher had taken her to Greece and Egypt, where they had witnessed the excavations at Luxor, and where the poet saw, with her friend's help, the visionary "writing on the wall" described in *Tribute to Freud*. For the rest of the poet's life, notwithstanding other entanglements on both sides, Bryher remained H.D.'s most stable friend and supporter. The "rescuing" women who appear in the three novellas of *Palimpsest* are based on Bryher; so, perhaps, are the supportive mother-goddesses of her late poems. The creative transformation which made those poems possible, however, is a mystery wrapped in the enigma of H.D.'s relation with Freud, about which much has been written and more is doubtless to come.[4]

According to *Tribute to Freud*, the primary motivation behind H.D.'s psychoanalytic sessions with "the Professor" in 1933–34 was her conviction that Europe was drifting toward a second war. Among her associates, she explains, "what I seemed to sense and wait for" was denied by one set and discussed in "predigested voluminous theories" by others. "One refused to admit the fact that the flood was coming—the other . . . didn't seem to have the very least idea of how to put the Ark together" (*Tribute*, pp. 85–86). "There was something that was beating in my brain. I do not say my heart—my brain. I wanted it to be let out. I wanted to dig down and dig out, root out my personal weeds, strengthen my purpose, reaffirm my beliefs, canalize my energies" in order to "fortify and equip myself to face war when it came, and to help in some subsidiary way, if my training were sufficient and my aptitudes suitable, with war-shocked and war-shattered people. . . . The thing I primarily wanted to fight in the open, war, its cause and effect, with its inevitable aftermath of neurotic breakdown and related nerve disorders" (*Tribute*, pp. 138–42).

It is not the usual reason for analysis. Nothing about H.D.'s relationship with Freud was usual, at least in her version of the story. For *Tribute* is an intricately layered document in which, just slightly below the surface account filled with reverence for "the blameless physician," lies a subtext rippling with subversion. H.D. speaks of herself as Freud's "student," boasts that he told her "you discovered for yourself what I discovered for the race," and hints that she flirted with him to the point of making him shout (her italics), "The trouble is—I am an old man—*you do not think it worth your while to love me.*" Upon this she comments solemnly, "Exactly it was as if the Supreme Being had hammered with his fist on the back of the couch," and also that Freud seemed "like a child hammering a porridge-spoon on the table." In one of the dreams they explicate together, an infant Moses is Freud, and H.D. is the watching sister Miriam. Elsewhere she tells of her fantasy of replacing a Promethean sibling. Analysis uncovers her yearning for union with her mother, and also her secret wish to become "the founder of a new religion." At times, the memoir makes clear, "the Professor was not always right," and she successfully defied him.

An overt issue was his disbelief, and her belief, in immortality. Behind this is H.D.'s need to define herself as a poet-prophet, for whom spiritual values were not illusion but central and valid reality; her tacit rejection of Freud's inclination to regard her visions—most especially her "writing on the wall" vision of a victorious goddess—as "dangerous symptoms," and an apparent refusal to take seriously his assumption that, like all women, what she primarily suffered from was the lack of a penis. In one of the book's more amusing *contretemps,* Freud hands her, saying it is the favorite among his treasures, a small bronze statue of Pallas Athene with one hand extended. " 'She is perfect,' he said, *'only she has lost her spear.'* " "I did not say anything," remarks H.D. These disagreements are hinted at with the greatest delicacy.

The poet's Freud was neither the religious skeptic nor the dogmatic believer in feminine inferiority and passivity, but the collector of sacred artifacts who was himself an "alchemist," a Thoth, a seerlike "hermit," a Hermes Trismegistus, an explorer of "the well of living waters" in men's souls. He was a prober into the human psyche who despite his doctrines had, H.D. insists, confirmed the validity of spiritual life and the creations that embody it, by discovering their source in man's unconscious life:

> He dared to say the dream came from an unexplored depth in man's consciousness . . . and the vast depth of that ocean was the same vast depth that to-day, as in Joseph's day, overflowing in man's small consciousness, produced inspiration, madness, creative idea or the dregs of the dreariest symptoms of mental unrest or disease. He had dared to . . . imply that this consciousness proclaimed all men one; all nations and races met in the universal world of the dream; and he had dared to say that the dream-symbol could be interpreted; its language, its imagery were common to the whole race not only of the living but of those ten thousand years dead.

Consequently, according to H.D., "man, understanding man, would save mankind." It is a conclusion the Freud of *Civilization and Its Discontents* would have scoffed at. However, what H.D. demanded of her teacher was an affirmation of her own certainty that by investigating the submerged life shadowed forth in dreams and associated "abnormal" mental states, one might not only achieve a personal health otherwise impossible. One might realize, through the cross-cultural universality of dream and myth images, mankind's actual unity, obscured beneath trivial surface dramas of individual and international conflict. Did H.D., then, charm the aging Freud, as a clever enough daughter can charm a father? Was he too old to resist her resistance? Is *Tribute* essentially a fiction, a myth, a "take" of the author's real mind which has taken twenty years to develop, in which Freud's rational authoritarian male force is slightly diminished, and his student's irrational feminine force is slightly augmented, so that they stand at last as playful equals, and the student gets, at last, her intellectual way?

As the book proceeds in its elusive, graceful, unchronological course, the image of Paradise plays an increasing part. This image is structurally opposed to the catastrophic stream of history, opposed to the morning after the *Kristallnacht* when H.D. followed chalked swastikas on the sidewalk to Freud's door, and the frightened servant whispered "but no-one has come to-day," and opposed to Freud's own doubt. Now that he has died, she wonders bemusedly how he felt when he woke and found himself immortal. She recalls how Freud once gave her a sprig of orange blossom sent by his son in the south of France. From this memory springs the poet's long closing meditation on Mignon's song—Mignon, Goethe's androgynous girl—"Kennst du das Land," where daughter leads father to Paradise.

She creates of him a father-figure, brother-figure, semi-lover and Muse. It is not important to know whether H.D.'s misreading of Freud is calculated or naive. It is to her purpose. He has led her to herself, she loves him, she leads him.

To understand what the poet means to say in her late poetry about myth and dream, time and history, war and poetry, there can be no better guidebook than *Tribute to Freud*. It is also the perfect introduction to her changed attitude toward authoritative men: profoundly needing their love and approval, impudently denying their authority, making muses not masters of them, even reinventing who they are.

VI.

How do we read the late H.D.? With the wind in our hair, a gleam in our eyes, and a sense of headlong forward motion. It

is motion, transformation and change that these poems are
about:

> In no wise is the pillar-of-fire
> that went before
>
> different from the pillar-of-fire
> that comes after;
>
> chasm, schism in consciousness
> must be bridged over;
>
> we are each, householder,
> each with a treasure;
>
> *The Walls Do Not Fall*

> I am not, nor mean to be
> the Daemon they made of me;
> going forward, my will was the wind.
>
> *Helen in Egypt*

Now the poems are not lapidary, not closed and finished ar-
tifacts containing tensions. There is a sense of lids sprung.
There is arrowy speed. Or the poem glides like a stream, cut-
ting the banks alongside it, apparently meandering but actu-
ally gravity-drawn and finding the swiftest possible route to its
ocean. "Resurrection is a sense of direction." Now the form is
not free verse but couplets in *Trilogy* and "Sagesse," triplets in
Helen in Egypt and its related love-epics "Hermetic Definition"
and "Winter Love," often with lovely chains of rhyme and off-
rhyme, as in the *fire-before-after-over-householder-treasure* se-
quence. The steady look of stanzas on the page visually gives a
sense of order and control, a spine, something to hold onto,
keel of canoe.

These constants are essential, because in other respects be-
sides the aesthetic and kinetic, the work will seem, to a begin-
ning reader, wildly confusing. Its apparently improvisational
"stream" of consciousness is fed by the poet's personal and
history's suprapersonal underground springs. Its logic is that
of psychoanalytic free association, which H.D. has adopted as a
governing principle of her poetics. Where it uses familiar tra-

ditions, classical or Christian, it transforms them. Part of the task H.D. sets herself is to recover the wholeness and continuity of what *Helen in Egypt* calls "all myth, the one reality," which involves locating Greek gods behind Christian, and Egyptian behind those; with them she conflates images from such branches of occult lore as alchemy, numerology, theosophy, cabbala. To a degree matched only by Blake's late prophecies, this poetry is psychodrama, not mimetic of what we usually call the "outside" or "real" world. Its characters are those who "know each other / by secret symbols / . . . we nameless initiates / born of one mother" who in *The Walls Do Not Fall* are civilization's spiritual seekers—and who may seem to exclude the ordinary reader rather firmly.

In another sense "the secret is no secret" (*Helen in Egypt*, p. 303) or is bones to philosophy but milk to faith. A student of mine reading the late H.D. told the class that it was the strangest thing: she didn't understand a word of what was going on, and yet she felt the poem had happened to her, somehow, was about something in her own life that she had forgotten. Others around the table nodded. H.D.'s ultimate subject is the shared human psyche, and her community of initiates potentially includes anyone who actively seeks personal integrity and the reunion of a divided self. So, although we cannot read H.D.'s late poetry rationally, we can read it with, as it were, our own dream-lives, our own "secret" knowledge of ourselves. Indeed, the poet insists on this:

> Now it appears very clear
> that the Holy Ghost,
>
> childhood's mysterious enigma
> is the Dream . . .
>
> open to everyone.
>
> *Trilogy,* p. 29

At this point H.D. diverges absolutely from Pound. Where he urges *books* as the path to wisdom, she urges, literally, *dreams.* For her insistence that dreams have a validity superceding the validity of books gives her the authority to reinvent reality, defying "civilization" and "history" as we have known them, from a subjectively female point of view. It is no accident that Pound's attention turned from Greece, a culture with remnants of Goddess-worship, to the exclusively male-oriented philosophy of Confucian China. H.D.'s mind at the same time sank like an anchor from Greece to Egypt and found Isis. From Isis it rose like a bubble and found Psyche "out of the cocoon," two mysteriously connected Marys in Christian myth, a Helen of Troy engaged in a quest of self-discovery, and a rainbow of goddesses who were projections of female love, wisdom, and creativity. Nor is it an accident that for Pound the ideal poetic language was the ideogram, where concrete visual surface and meaning are (or so he argued) identical and accessible to the objective intellect, while H.D.'s paradigm of poetic language became Helen's Egyptian hieroglyph, where meaning is hidden inside the visual image and can only be deciphered when she discovers that "she herself is the writing."

The immediate intention of *The Walls Do Not Fall*, written in London during the Blitz of 1944, was to defy the Sword with the Word. H.D. and Bryher had chosen to live in London during this second war specifically to confront "the thing I wanted to fight in the open, war, its cause and effects." Thus at the opening of *Walls*, bombed buildings recall the ruined shrine at Karnak, roofless and desolate, but this parallel reminds her that "gods have been smashed before / and idols and their secret is stored / in man's very speech." The idea of writing endures "though our books are a floor / of smoldering ash under our feet." There exists a living continuity between ancient and modern gods, and an equally living need of civilization for its "scribes." In the combat of war against faith, destruction against creation, the poet must struggle, and *Walls* is the record of a sometimes despairing struggle, toward a rejection of chronology and linear narrative, a stilling of jeering external voices and internal fears, before her personal reconstructive visions can crystallize.

What gradually emerges in *Trilogy* is that H.D.'s poetry-versus-war strategy involves not only faith that reality is ultimately spiritual and subjective instead of material and time-trapped. It also involves the imagining of a feminine reality strong enough to counterbalance male power and authority in the poet's own mind. Instead of the innocent androgyny of the early work and the sexual polarization of her middle period, there is a steady drift in *Trilogy* from traditional male-centeredness to radical female-centeredness. The most obvious form this takes is the progress of the sacred epiphanies which produce the climactic moments of these poems.

In *Walls* she dreams of the god Amen-Christos, whom she is barely able to disentangle from the "junk-shop" images of a corrupted Christianity, and whom she begs, "Take me home, take me home." In *Tribute to the Angels*, H.D.'s tacit revision of the seven apocalyptic angels in Revelation, which places the angel of war in a larger cycle which it cannot dominate, is interrupted by the dream of a Lady who appears to be the feminine equivalent of the transfigured Christ. The Lady can be interpreted by nobody but the poet, for whom she includes and transcends classical and Christian iconography: the volume in the Lady's hand "is not the tome of the ancient wisdom" but "the unwritten volume of the new." Finally in *The Flowering of the Rod*, the poet leaves the "place-of-a-skull" and "the bitter unending wars" behind:

> I go where I love and where I am loved,
> into the snow;
>
> I go to the things I love
> with no thought of duty or pity;

and moves toward the vision of the mystic Magdalen. As if she were a racehorse inspirited by the leaping of each successive hurdle, the poet's tone grows happier and more confident with each apparition, more ready to challenge old notions, until in *Flowering* she boldly places her image of female significance in the mind of a Magus, a traditional "wise" man whose initial response to the Magdalen's visit is:

it was unseemly that a woman
appear disordered, disheveled

it was unseemly that a woman
appear at all.

Mary has come to obtain from Kaspar the myrrh with which
she will anoint Christ's feet—and Mary-myrrh is a pun the poet
repeats, making clear it is herself she is giving to God. What
Kaspar obtains from her, on the other hand, is revelation. His
rationality and misogyny are a mental "citadel" that falls dur-
ing the split-second when he experiences a point of light on
Mary's hair as a vision culminating in "the whole scope and
plan" of paradise. He sees images of three women, the Mag-
dalen's "daimons," and in the headband-jewel of one of them
he sees the islands and cities of the blest:

and what he saw made his heart so glad
that it was as if he suffered,

his heart labored so
with his ecstasy.

And when H.D. remarks, as if she were perusing rabbinic
texts, that Kaspar's identity is uncertain, "some say he was an
old lover . . . some say he was Abraham,/ some say he was
God," it is one of her little jokes. For if Mary is certainly H.D.,
embarrassing everyone by "actually kissing" her lord's feet—

the first actually to witness His life-after-death
was an unbalanced, neurotic woman . . .

I am Mary, she said, of Magdala,
I am Mary, a great tower . . .

—then just as certainly Kaspar is Freud, and the poet is gently
turning the tables on the masculine authority she had needed
to define her.

The imagery H.D. uses to symbolize poetry also shifts dur-
ing the course of *Trilogy*. "The sceptre, the rod of power," the

healing "Caduceus" and even "the stylus . . . the pen, the quill" in *Walls* are consciously phallic. Then come the feminine images, organic and uterine: the poet's imagination as shell-fish, indigestible by whales, begetting pearl; or as worm, clinging persistently to grassblade, becoming a cocoon-wrapped potential butterfly (we remember that the butterfly is Psyche, the Soul conceived as a girl in love with Eros); or as a "cup" trying to contain the water that will turn to wine; or as an "urn" in which a seed of faith sprouts into a tree of life. Words themselves take on a feminine character:

> they are anagrams, cryptograms
> little boxes, conditioned
>
> to hatch butterflies.

In *Tribute to the Angels,* as the sexuality of the symbolism heightens, words for bitterness and sea-brine are melted in the "bowl" of an alchemist's crucible, making "mer, mere, mère, mater . . . Mary, / Star of the Sea," who is Virgin, Venus and Astarte. In *Flowering,* both poetry and the mysterious feminine continuum are symbolized by the fragrant myrrh sealed in a jar, and the poet's art of fusion is such that in the final nativity scene at Bethlehem it appears, as we gaze through Kaspar's wondering eyes, that the myrrh can be Mary's self, the baby in her arms, and the poem we are completing.[5]

Even more explicitly than *Trilogy, Helen in Egypt* redefines the relationship of Woman to "the iron-ring" of War, with the Trojan War standing as prototype not only for all historic conflict but for all failures in human self-knowledge. Here H.D. stresses the idea of woman's position as sacrificial victim of male violence, crystallized in the figures of Helen, blamed for the war and "hated of all Greece," and Iphigenia, slaughtered so that the ships could sail to Troy. To Achilles, the archetypal warrior, woman is either sexual spoils or an impediment to the life of male-oriented heroism:

> The Command was bequest from the past,
> from father to son,

the Command bound past to the present

and the present to aeons to come,
the Command was my father, my brother,
my lover, my God.

In the romance between Helen and Achilles, the moment of
erotic ecstasy for her comes as his attempt to strangle her turns
magically to lovemaking:

> *O Thetis, O sea-mother,*
> I prayed, as he clutched my throat
>
> with his fingers' remorseless steel,
> *let me go out, let me forget,*
> *let me be lost . . . .*
>
> *O Thetis, O sea-mother,* I prayed under his cloak,
> *let me remember, let me remember,*
> *forever, this Star in the night.*

This exactly parallels Sylvia Plath's insight that "every woman
adores a Fascist," and yet it is quite different.

Helen of Troy's literary history is that of wife and mistress.
But for H.D., woman-as-erotic-object has become woman-as-
subject, engaged in a triple quest: to gain spiritual knowledge
which will "reconcile Trojan and Greek," Greek and Egyptian
gods and cultures; to "fight for Helena," reintegrating a splin-
tered identity scarred by men's hatred; and to reconstruct a
spiritual family including parents, siblings, lover, children. She
is aided by the god Amen-Zeus, the goddess Isis-Thetis-Aph-
rodite, and the supportive father figure and fellow-quester
Theseus (another version of Freud). She is above all a seeker of
enlightenment, much like her creator, and like H.D., is men-
tally satisfied by discovering unities in dualities. Thus the Hel-
en-Achilles coupling, embedded in the larger plot, is an out-
come of "love's arrow" destroying the hero's invulnerability
and will to power, and gradually restoring an emotional link
with a lost feminine self whose "eidolon" is his mother Thetis.
For Helen, the pairing with her polar opposite eventually re-
leases a "heroic" self, whom the spectacle of conflict excites

instead of frightens. We have, then, H.D.'s old dream of "man-woman," "woman-man," the balanced opposites. Like Isis-Osiris and Aphrodite-Ares, of whom they are mortal avatars, Helen and Achilles produce a child, who represents the rebirth of their two child-selves: wild Helen, before she was anyone's wife or mistress, and Achilles, his mother's son, before he was anyone's soldier.

H.D. called *Helen in Egypt* her "Cantos," and one can imagine *Trilogy* and *Helen* eventually taking their places somewhere near *Four Quartets* and Pound's *Cantos*, in that infinitely readjustable order—something like a large dinner party—which T. S. Eliot tells us the monuments of great literature together compose. The Christianity of *Trilogy* would of course be very different from Eliot's, being less concerned with sin and self-surrender, more with ecstasy and rebirth, though both are poems about faith's survival in times of apocalyptic destruction and intellectual nihilism. And H.D.'s works would differ from both *Cantos* and *Quartets* in their degree of inwardness, their rejection of outer authority, or rather their painstaking insistence on transforming what was "beautiful yet static, empty/old thought, old convention" (*Trilogy*, p. 26) into personal revelation. As for the three amazing pieces of *Hermetic Definition*, written in the last four years of H.D.'s life: these I would place near *Desert Music* and "Asphodel, That Greeny Flower."

What Norman Holmes Pearson sees in *Hermetic Definition* is the quest of Psyche for Eros: "Women are individually seeking, as one woman, fragments of the Eternal Lover. As the Eternal Lover has been scattered or dissociated, so she in her search for him." True but not the whole truth. In the volume's title poem the ailing seventy-year-old poet's absurd infatuation with a handsome young "amber-eyed" Haitian journalist becomes, when he is contemptuous of her writing and fails to answer her letters, a difficult "condition." She sustains herself by obeying a mysterious goddess who commands "*write, write or die.*" (Shall I say that I personally find this poem both embarrassing and marvelous? That I want to avert my eyes from the painful, ridiculous self-defeating spectacle of the old lady throwing herself at the young man? And that something in me applauds this persistence, remembering her epithets for Aphrodite, "shameless and radiant?") Nine months after their meeting come the young man's sudden death of a heart attack, and the completed poem, structured in sections equivalent to the trimesters of pregnancy, apotheosizing his "birth" as an avatar of Osiris. A remarkable conception.

In the second poem of *Hermetic Definition,* "Sagesse," there is again a presiding goddess. "Wisdom" is imprisoned and disguised as the ungainly Scops Owl in the London Zoo, like the poet immobilized in the hospital at Zurich with a broken hip. She is simultaneously the *Grand Mer* (pun on great sea—great mother—grandmother) patroness and protectress of the poet engaged in occult study and "giving my life force to these little songs." The charming poem-within-a-poem of "Sagesse" concerns a little working-class London girl whose family has survived the Blitz and who is "took queer" by the owl, unconsciously recognizing its sacredness. This lovely "child" of H.D.'s imagination is so plainly the girl Hilda Doolittle reborn in apocalyptic times that reading "Sagesse" is like witnessing a kind of poetic parthenogenesis.

"Sagesse" has a quality of purity and joy that links it with H.D.'s earliest lyrics, but it is far more tender. Significantly, I think, there is no strong male principle in this poem, and all the London characters who remember the war seem to have been schooled by it into an earnest kindliness that enables them to love one another and to support the lonely, latently visionary little girl. But this vision of communal gentleness is not the poet's final formulation. "Winter Love," composed in the early months of 1959, returns to the theme of sexual polarity and the powerlessness of women. The poem is at once a coda to *Helen in Egypt* and a poetic reinvention of H.D.'s newly finished memoir of Pound, *End to Torment.* Helen-H.D. is now linked to Odysseus-Pound. The link is tragic. An old Helen, abandoned by all previous loves, recalls an ancient unsatisfied romance with Odysseus back in her Spartan girlhood. She imagines a reunion, which would compensate her losses and cancel the disaster of the Trojan War and all wars. At the nadir of the poem she bitterly acknowledges that this is an illusion, that "Helen is deserted utterly."

But the conclusion of "Winter Love" describes a reality generated by an illusion. It is another child. Or it is a poem. To give birth to it is exhausting labor. "Grandam, midwife, *Sage-Femme* / let me rest, let me rest, / I can't struggle any more." *Sage-Femme*, literally "wise woman," is French for "midwife," a homely incarnation of H.D.'s mother-goddess in keeping with the authenticity of the birth scene over which she presides. When the child-poem is born, H.D. at first resists giving suck to this soft but ruthless being whose feeding is the infant version of the lover's lust:

> I am delirious now and mean to be,
> the whole earth shudders with my ecstasy,
> take *Espérance* away;
>
> cruel, cruel *Sage-Femme*,
> to place him in my arms,
> cruel, cruel *Grande Dame*,
>
> to pull my tunic down,
> so Odysseus sought my breast
> with savage kiss;
>
> cruel, cruel midwife,
> so secretly to steal my phantom self,
> my invisibility, my hopelessness, my fate . . .

But her breasts sweetly swell with what "must be given" to Hope. The poem and the volume conclude: "*Espérance*, O golden bee, / take life afresh and if you must, / so slay me."

"O golden bee." It is the Eros of *Hymen*, alive after forty years. It is also any newborn, or any poem. To me this final lyric of "Winter Love" is astonishing. How did the old lady remember so vividly the sensations of a new mother, at the point where she is pulled equally by death and life? How did she contrive to fuse the triple themes of feminine sexuality, creativity and procreativity so seamlessly at last?

One must recall again her stubbornness. At the advent of her final period, early in *The Walls Do Not Fall,* H.D. announces it:

> In me (the worm) clearly
> is no righteousness but this—
>
> persistence.

By persistence H.D. became the first poet in our history to create poetic myths centered on a feminine principle, in which male figures play the kinds of roles females have always played in male myths. To the heroine, man is desired, and feared; he is father, lover, brother, infant; she herself must define his nature while she defines her own. What the female principle meant to H.D., above all, was love and unity: "chasm, schism in consciousness / must be bridged over"; division, fragmentation must be healed. She is the single one among the Moderns who begins poems with death and ends them with birth. It is appropriate that H.D. is our first poet to imagine a female being in whom a biological life, a life of feeling, and a life of dedicated spirituality and artistic creation are not divided but one.

NOTES

1. H.D.'s poetry has been notoriously difficult to obtain. The *Selected Poems* published by Grove Press in 1957 is thin and unrepresentative. The beautiful 1925 *Collected Poems of H.D.* (reprint ed., New York: Boni and Liveright, 1940) contains poems collected from her first three volumes, as well as several translations. *Hippolytus Temporizes* (Boston: Houghton Mifflin, 1927) and *Red Roses for Bronze* (London: Chatto and Windus, 1931; Boston: Houghton Mifflin, 1931) are also important for her middle period. The long late works, *Trilogy, Helen in Egypt* and *Hermetic Definition,* are readily available, happily, from New Directions.

   H.D.'s prose is another question. Several works of fiction appeared in her lifetime; some remain unpublished. I have made use of the early novel *Her* (published under the title *HERmione* by New Directions, 1981); *Palimpsest,* which contains the three related novellas "Hipparchia," "Murex," and "Secret Name" (Boston: Houghton Mifflin, 1926); and *Bid Me to Live* (*A Madrigal*) (Grove Press, 1960). In addition, *Tribute to Freud* (McGraw-Hill, 1974) is a masterpiece, and *End to Torment: A Memoir of Ezra Pound* (New Directions, 1979) is a valuable account of Pound's literary and erotic importance to H.D.

2. Pound's idea of the experiential basis of mythology, in "Psychology and the Troubadours," is quoted by George Kearns, *Guide to Ezra Pound's Selected Cantos* (New Brunswick, N.J.: Rutgers University Press, 1980), p. 28. Pound's "Religio or the Child's Guide to Knowledge" appeared in *Pavannes and Divisions,* and is reprinted in *Selected Prose, 1909–1965,* ed. William Cookson (London: Faber and Faber, 1973), p. 47.

3. For the term "romantic thralldom," and a sense of the importance of this theme in H.D.'s life and work, I am indebted to Rachel DuPlessis, "Romantic Thralldom in H.D.," *Contemporary Literature* (Spring 1979):178–203.

4. The Autumn 1969 issue of *Contemporary Literature,* devoted to H.D. (and a splendid source of material about her), includes two brilliant but subtly condescending, psychoanalytically-oriented essays on the poet: Joseph N. Riddel's "H.D. and the Poetics of 'Spiritual Realism,'" and Norman Holland's "H.D. and the 'Blameless Physician.'" My own sense of the H.D.-Freud connection derives largely from Susan Friedman, *Psyche Reborn: The Emergence of H.D.* (Bloomington: Indiana University Press, 1981). This book is an indispensable introduction to H.D.'s poetry, especially her late work. And for the initiate, there is Robert Duncan's beautiful work-in-progress, *The H.D. Book*—of which the pieces are presently as scattered as the limbs of Osiris himself. See, however, the section of it in *Montemora* 8 (1981):79–113, for a view of Freud as visionary as H.D.'s. Duncan is certainly H.D.'s most kindred spirit among poets writing today.

5. A fine essay on this difficult poem is Susan Gubar's "The Echoing Spell of H.D.'s *Trilogy*" in *Shakespeare's Sisters,* eds. Sandra M. Gilbert and Susan Gubar (Bloomington: Indiana University Press, 1979).

The Americanization of Sylvia

Sylvia Plath's first published book of poems, *The Colossus* (1960), received the mild critical commendation usually accruing to competent, promising, and rather mediocre first books. Her second, appearing posthumously after her suicide in 1963, provoked a violent and brief literary cultism, some highly excited critical acclaim and nervous critical attack,[1] and a rain of elegies and tributes by fellow poets. Since many of the poems in *Ariel* deal, directly and passionately, with illness, death, suicide and rage, it is not surprising that commentary on Plath typically identifies her poetry with her biography, declaring, for example, that "the long, escalating drive toward suicide and the period of extraordinary creativity . . . actually coincided . . . or were at least two functions of the same process."[2]

In this respect sophisticated critics resemble naive readers. I have refereed more than one angry classroom debate between Plath defenders and Plath antagonists in which it was perfectly clear that the issue was the morality of suicide. Had the poet the "right" to kill herself? Was she "self-indulgent?" The questions can of course be pushed further. Was her death society's fault, for romanticizing "extremism" and burn-out in artists? Was it Otto Plath's fault, for being an authoritarian papa and inscribing feminine passivity upon his little daughter forever? Should we blame the self-sacrificing Aurelia Plath for being a model of wifely submissiveness and because she forced Sylvia to become the appallingly and unrelievedly enthusiastic-and-grateful-and-happy American Girl of *Letters Home?* Was it that the "absolutely white person" (see "In Plaster") of Sylvia's social facade was so unyielding and disruption-proof as to press all antisocial impulses back into the private self, where they rankled and festered? Or did Sylvia create the Good Girl mask because she herself feared volcanic forces within? Did Ted Hughes really kill Sylvia? ("But she *picked* him," half the class leaps to remark.) What if we shift our camera backward from this particular life, until we see Plath sharing a frame with other inconsolable children, such as Hemingway and Berryman, who were perhaps doomed from the moment of their fathers' suicides, though they fought fate as long as they were able? Think of that old notion of the curse on a family, so central to Greek tragedy. Or the Old Testament remonstrance: "The fathers have eaten sour grapes, and the children's teeth are set on edge." We would love to refute that, if we could. Or, shifting still further back, must we ask if some people are congenital emotional hemophiliacs—if you cut them they cannot make scar tissue, they simply keep bleeding—and if so, what is the connection between such a condition and the genesis of poetry?

I do not think such questions are improper, provided we see how the multiplicity of answers must lead us finally to a sense of mystery. We do not know why some people destroy themselves, just as we do not know why some people destroy others. "Why look'st thou so?" asks the wedding guest. "With my crossbow I shot the Albatross," replies the Ancient Mariner. Consequences follow, but why did he shoot it? Coleridge cannot say. Our frustrated wish to clear up the mystery and label the package "Someone Else: Not Me" might lead us to understand that what we are really asking about is our own agitation. This too is proper. No failure to distinguish art from life is quite so stupid as pretending that poetry is some kind of sterile swabbed tissue of language uninfected by the poet's life and incapable of infecting the reader's life.

My own response, on first reading *Ariel,* was a thought compounded of something like *Good God, it's real* and *Damn, she did it*—as if having "done it" were a triumph—and a physical sensation like that of being slapped hard: rush of adrenalin, stunned amazement. I was stealing time to read. In those days I stole whatever time I could from the demands of family and the demands of freshman classes. Either set of duties was inherently infinite, infinitely guilt-producing. Often it seemed I never slept. It was very late, my husband and two babies were asleep, it was icy and windy outside the apartment as I sat under the lamp and moaned my way through poems written in the hours before the sound of the milkman and the cries of children, during the last six months of Plath's life.

If I ask myself in retrospect precisely what I mean by *Damn, she did it*, the answer is complex ("like everything else," as the poet herself might observe). Most obviously: she had dared to kill herself, as in all probability I never would. This made her somehow an aristocrat and me a peasant gasping at her nobility. Of course I too wanted annihilation. Second: she had permitted herself emotions which for me were forbidden, and which I spent a considerable amount of effort attempting to repress. Self-loathing, that drug. Loathing of others, especially my near and dear. Desire to kill as well as die. Fury of the trapped animal. Plenty of TNT in that kitchen cabinet. The authenticity of this poet's hatreds was for me nailed down of course by their rootedness in a feminine body and their location among domestic arrangements. It was justified by her terror and anger at war and her sense of helplessness in the face of brutality, which I shared and share. I also shared her understanding of maternal love and ecstasy in poems like "Morning Song" or "Balloons," her fierce grasp of life in poems like "Tulips," the celebration of womanhood and rebirth that closes the bee poems (which, by the way, Hughes tells us were originally intended to conclude *Ariel* itself; for unspecified reasons he moved these poems away from the manuscript's close, thus altering its emotional plotline).[3] The fact that this woman knew the nature of specific female pleasures, however tenuously, however they failed to save her, made the downward spin of her whirlpool even more seductive to my mind.

And then: as a poet, oh, as a poet, she had done it. She had contrived not merely to feel freely but to state clearly. As a poet, greedy, I wanted her bag of tricks.

Fifteen years later I resemble Sylvia less than I first imagined. In middle age I am a peasant, thick-skinned and concerned with survival, in a way that the sensitive young woman I was could not have anticipated. I want to live to be a hundred. I see myself wrinkled and sage, dropping off the branch in the ultramarine cold, very late in the season, a twilight scene with snow flurries. But to my first encounter with Plath I date the initial stirrings of a realization (practical not theoretical, and not her realization but mine) that to accomplish this intention will require, for me, reconciliation with a self that wants to kill or die. Not denial, not "indulgence": reconciliation. It is an understanding I share with many other women, taught by Plath to recognize the underside of our womanly propriety. At the same moment as we are pulling ourselves from martyrdom's shadows to some sort of daylight, we honor her for being among the first to run a flashlight over the cave walls.

But it is the bag of tricks, the art, that I still admire unreservedly, having found it inimitable. Or rather I should say I found it impossible to steal from and get away with, since a Plath device in someone else's poem can be spotted miles off, like a giraffe meandering over tundra. And what strikes me now, reading through Plath's *Collected Poems,* is how she achieved a voice that is not only distinctly her own but distinctly American, through an almost complete reversal of stylistic direction. For the weakness of Plath's earliest work is that it is derivative and safe in style if not substance; and the strength of the poetry from 1960 on is achieved by means of a technique that has nothing to do with safety, everything to do with risk.

The American grain Plath belongs to is that part of our writing which, since the nineteenth century, has been deliberately antibelletristic, deliberately naive, programmatically occupied with climbing over the enclosures of established forms, and perpetually reinsisting that the true function of the writer is the documentation of physical and emotional facts, in a fashion as close to journalism as possible. Has any other nation produced so many major writers who started out as journalists? At any rate, from Whitman's installation of the muse amid the kitchenware to Williams' filthy Passaic, from Melville's encyclopedic turgidity to Hemingway's "true" sentence, from *Walden* to *Let Us Now Praise Famous Men*—and consider writers like Twain, Sherwood Anderson, Ring Lardner, John Dos Passos, E. A. Robinson, Edgar Lee Masters, Carl Sandburg, Robert Frost, to name at random a few majors and minors and indicate the boundaries—the native American tradition continually produces writers who write as if art were literally supposed to represent life without falsification, and as if it were preferable to have real toads at the expense of imaginary gardens. An example: "I went to the woods because I wished to live deliberately, to front only the essential facts of life," says Thoreau in *Walden,* "to shave close, to drive life into a corner and reduce it to its lowest terms, and, if it proved to be mean, why then to get the whole and genuine meanness of it and publish its meanness to the world; or if it were sublime, to know it by experience, and be able to give a true account of it in my next excursion."

Most nineteenth-century Americans, including Thoreau, favored the sublime. Emerson did not choose to suppose that the transparent eyeball would ever behold anything displeasing. Whitman acknowledged that to face Fact meant to face Death, but tried to be cheerful about it. Intimations of the whole and genuine meanness surface only occasionally, in Melville, the later Twain, and Dickinson. Think of Dickinson's "I heard a fly buzz," or "the sky is low, the clouds are mean," or the bird on her garden walk who "bit an Angleworm in halves / And ate the fellow, raw." Meanness is a dominant twentieth- rather than nineteenth-century convention. Yet even Thoreau remarks characteristically, a few lines after the passage I have just quoted, "If you stand right fronting and face to face to a fact, you will see the sun glimmer on both its surfaces, as if it were a cimeter, and feel its sweet edge dividing you through the heart and marrow, and so you will happily conclude your mortal career. Be it life or death, we crave only reality. If we are really dying, let us hear the rattle in our throats and feel cold in the extremities; if we are alive, let us go about our business." Notice, now, the striking resemblance between Thoreau's image of the lethal swordlike "fact" and the conclusion of *Ariel*'s "A Birthday Present," in which the unopened gift is also a desired, unconfronted fact:

> Only let down the veil, the veil, the veil.
> If it were death
>
> I would admire the deep gravity of it, its timeless eyes.
> I would know you were serious.
>
> There would be a nobility then, there would be a birthday.
> And the knife not carve but enter
>
> Pure and clean as the cry of a baby
> And the universe slide from my side.

Or compare Thoreau's not quite serious recommendation, "If we are really dying, let us hear the rattle in our throats and feel cold in the extremities," with Plath's "Dying / Is an art, like everything else. / I do it exceptionally well. / I do it so it feels like hell. / I do it so it feels real." And compare both with Dickinson's "I like a look of Agony, / Because I know it's true."

The difference between *The Colossus* and *Ariel* lies in the poet's advancing will and ability to do it, technically, so it feels real, without veils. If Plath commits herself in her first book to "tending, without stop, the blunt / Indefatigible fact," ("Night Shift") she often fails. It is not a question of themes, which are implicitly as brutal in *The Colossus* as in *Ariel*. Several of the poems in *Ariel* are precisely re-visions of poems in *The Colossus*. The astonishing change occurs in the typical occasions employed, the diction, and the form of the poems. One could summarize the change by saying that having learned to see the skull beneath the skin, she threw away the skin.

The first book is safer in many ways. It depends on past tradition, and this is not simply a matter of allusions to classical and European literature and art, although the allusions are there. It obeys, as most academic poetry in the fifties did, that line of T. S. Eliot's criticism which cautions severely against the shallowness of merely personal ideas, and reasonably asserts that writing which assimilates the past can have a philosophical assurance, a firmness and density of texture, otherwise unavailable. Poems like "The Manor Garden," "Two Views of a Cadaver Room" (one view is in a medical school, the other a Breughel painting), "Hardcastle Crags," "Point Shirley," "Watercolor of Grantchester Meadows," and others, as their titles indicate, hang themselves onto places, or works of art or architecture. They are descriptive-meditative poems, out of Wordsworth by Auden or Lowell. They have a distance, usually, a sense of meditation completed. They seem assured, stable, controlled. Some of the more personally analytical—or psychotic—pieces such as "The Thin People" or "The Disquieting Muses" in *The Colossus* fail to follow this line. And the poet throws it off in *Ariel,* retaining nothing bookish or archaic-sounding beyond a few titles and a few minor references. For Plath, who had been so earnestly the good student, the sincere imitator "adhering to rules, to rules, to rules," it is a radical break.

Is the loss of density and firmness worth it? Compare the first book's poems about her father, "The Colossus" and "Full Fathom Five," with the later "Daddy." The titles tell all. The earlier poems have some strength and passion, but also a saving, self-protective primness. Father is a shattered statue, or a submerged kingly titan. The "archaic trenched lines / Of your grained face shed time in runnels." He is formally addressed: "O father, all by yourself / You are pithy and historical as the Roman Forum," or "Old Man, you surface seldom." There is a lyricized death wish, "Your shelled bed I remember. / Father, this thick air is murderous. / I would breathe water," and a classicizing scorn, "Perhaps you consider yourself an oracle, / Mouthpiece of the dead, or of some god or other." Well and good, but not the same thing as "You do not do, you do not do / Any more, black shoe / In which I have lived like a foot." Or "At twenty I tried to die / To get back, back, back to you. / I thought even the bones would do." Or a more contemporary historical (not literary) accusation, "Not God but a swastika . . . Every woman adores a Fascist / The boot in the face."

In the earlier poems some hard language loses its bite because of the distance imposed by an objective tone, allusion used only as illustration, and the fact that the ironies are lavished on easy game, not yet turned against the poet herself. In the later poems (as these quotations only begin to indicate) hysteria veiled becomes hysteria unveiled, what it feels like, without logical development or analysis, self-indulgent, regressive, shrilly repetitive, exaggerated—and of course ultimately pathetic, ultimately ridiculous, like a child having a tantrum. Think of the bravado of that last line: "Daddy, Daddy, you bastard, I'm through," where "through" should mean she has successfully punctured him ("a stake in your fat black heart"), is finished with her attachment to him, and has emerged from something like a tunnel. We believe her not at all. The more she screams the more we know she will never be through. It is the same with the famous ending of "Lady Lazarus," where the poet warns she will rise from the dead and "eat men like air." That men do dread the avenging maenad Plath evokes here is unquestionable. At the same time, her incantation is hollow. She is impersonating a female phoenix-fiend like a woman wearing a Halloween costume, or a child saying "I'll kill you" to the grownups, or Lear bellowing "I will do such things—/ What they are yet I know not, but they shall be / The terrors of the earth." She is powerless, she knows it, she hates it. The reader may fear, but must also pity.

"Daddy" and "Lady Lazarus" are typical, for the "I" at the center of an *Ariel* poem is commonly childish and incomplete, moving the poem along by sheer will, and forcing the reader into disequilibrium. At times the reader may be forced to identify with Plath's antagonists, the loving tormentors against whom certain poems are acts of fury. "You" are the leering crowd craving a look at her scars, you are Herr Doktor, Herr Enemy, you are the husband whose cool normality is killing her, you are the inane lady friends, the obscenely clinging mother in "Medusa," you are Daddy. This combination of a refusal of a traditional literary locus, dramatic and arrogant assertion of a self which is totally unstable but is the only self she has, and enraged attack on an outside world seen as stupidly and brutally stable, produces a poetry which continually threatens to slide into absurdity.

She undertakes a similar gamble with her language. In *The Colossus*, the language is neutrally literary (with complex sentences, parallelisms, inversions, compound epithets) most of the time, privately symbolic (rather like early Roethke) some of the time, colloquial occasionally and in the best pieces. In *Ariel*, the American language rises gap-toothed from the waves. It is brusque, businesslike, and bitchy. It deflates everything it touches. It grins behind and through the literary language, exploiting it. It makes a wife-to-be:

> A living doll, everywhere you look.
> It can sew, it can cook,
> It can talk, talk, talk . . .
> You have a hole, it's a poultice.
> You have an eye, it's an image.
> My boy, it's your last resort.
>
> ["The Applicant"]

It explains abortive suicide:

> I have done it again.
> One year in every ten
> I manage it—
> A sort of walking miracle, my skin
> Bright as a Nazi lampshade . . .
> My face a featureless, fine
> Jew linen.
>
> ["Lady Lazarus"]

It disposes of a lady friend's advice:

> You say I should drown the kittens. Their smell!
> You say I should drown my girl . . .
> I should sit on a rock off Cornwall and comb my hair.
> I should wear tiger pants, I should have an affair.
> We should meet in another life, we should meet in air,
> Me and you.
>
> ["Lesbos"]

It responds to a cut:

> What a thrill—
> My thumb instead of an onion.
>
> ["Cut"]

As a version of Donne's "Therefore ask not . . . It tolls for thee," it summarizes:

> The dead bell.
> The dead bell.
> Somebody's done for.
>
> ["Death & Co."]

"Doomed" would have been the obvious "literary" word here; "done for" does not so much evoke *timor mortis* as express contempt for literature alongside the dread of death.

Here the gain is clear, since everybody likes the shock of recognition from a good mimesis of the spoken tongue. Novelists with an ear for idiom will sell. Playwrights who have it will prosper. But there is an equivalent risk. Colloquial meat decays—nobody cares how people talked twenty years ago—and the only thing that can preserve it fresh is salt. Readers apparently *remain* delighted with language such as men did use, if and only if it is funny, or its author ironic. Where Plath's colloquialism is "straight" it will probably dissolve shortly into its English background, having served its purpose of helping her write the tongue she spoke, and leaving poems perhaps a little thinner than they needed to be. It will be a permanent asset, I would guess, in the poems where it turns most spitefully against itself—"The Applicant," "Lady Lazarus," "Cut," "Death & Co.," "Lesbos," "A Birthday Present," "Daddy"—as if to prove that a world which talks like this, therefore thinks like this, therefore is like this, shallow and nasty, cannot deserve one's survival.

This ironic streak, in *Ariel,* even engages itself to something as technical as prosody. Plath's musical ear, like her ear for vernacular, is dead keen. Yet in her early work it seems to function almost decoratively rather than organically. Meter in

The Colossus is usually fairly loose, rhymes fashionably false, and so on. But the prosodically conscious reader is led to play can-you-find-this, as in a picture puzzle book: terza rima in "Sow," "Lorelei," "Full Fathom Five," "Man in Black," "Snake-charmer," "Medallion," rime royale in "The Eye-Mote," three-line *a*-rhyme stanza in "Bull of Bandylaw," couplets in "The Thin People," all cleverly disguised, lines broken with apparent irregularity turning out time after time to serve complicated and static stanza patterns. *Ariel* is less patient. Poems drop into and out of formal verse as if time were too dear to spend rewriting. If something happens to fall into meter, fine. If it doesn't, the devil with it. This is a free verse always approaching the older, stricter discipline, and gaining power from the tension. But the rationale of free verse in *Ariel* is not just a matter of variety, speaking voice, or even asserted emotionalism, but an attraction-repulsion toward formality as if to write the perfectly polished, formal poem would be to die. The verse correlates with her scorn, or fear, of everything orderly and finished, and with her paradoxically simultaneous feeling that the moment of death, which is her epitome of total organization, is desirable. In "Berck-Plage," she explains about an old man's sheeted corpse, "This is what it is to be complete. It is horrible." A few lines later she declares, "It is a blessing, it is a blessing." Similarly, her repeated device of carrying rhymes and assonances over irregularly from stanza to stanza, instead of enclosing them within stanza units, reinforces a cultivation of speed-effects which is also paradoxical. She explains that "what I love is / The piston in motion"; yet the various journeys she undertakes in this book by spiritual horse or nightmare rail, while they seem, in violent motion, the antithesis of death's static perfection, inevitably turn out to be hurtling as fast as they can toward the point of extinction.

This connection between the idea of dying and the idea of formal beauty explains why Plath's most conspicuously musical moments tend to be the most annihilating. A curious thing happens in several of the poems, where she will seem to be talking around and about, and then suddenly hit her stride and go by like a blue streak. The mechanics of this effect of intensification involve alliterations, assonances, and rhymes coming fast and repeatedly, and the echoes of sound reinforcing semantic links—sometimes accretively, as in "The flesh the grave cave ate" or "How you jump . . . "Thumb stump," or more subtly in the close of *Ariel*'s title poem, which may be about a runaway horse (as we have been told) or may be about masturbation:

I

Foam to wheat, a glitter of seas.
The child's cry
Melts in the wall,
And I
Am the arrow,

The dew that flies,
Suicidal, at one with the drive
Into the red
Eye, the cauldron of morning.

Or sometimes the echoes work ironically, as in the lines from "Lady Lazarus" which I have already quoted, where the terms *well, hell, real, feels, call,* all have their meanings viciously transformed by each other's presence:

Dying
Is an art, like everything else.
I do it exceptionally well.
I do it so it feels like hell.
I do it so it feels real.
I guess you could say I've a call.

If meter and rhyme in these poems forfeit their usual function of providing part of a consistent sense of decorous normality in poetry, or retain suggestions of order and beauty only to reveal the poet's terror of order and beauty, Plath's late imagery similarly avoids decorativeness, and sometimes forfeits coherence, for the sake of truth to the immediately experienced private fact. Plath's imagery is commonly considered her greatest asset, and is often labelled "striking," which misses the point that the virtue of an image, in poetry or elsewhere, consists minimally in its novelty, maximally in its accuracy. Some of the effects that had the strongest impact on me on first reading—the restriction of her spectrum to primary colors, the harping on white for purity and death, red for life and violence, the obsession with objects that are bare and bald, the sinister smiles, the embodied bones and hair—seem in retrospect weak and formulaic. Where Plath's imagery is genuinely powerful it is because the poet is fixing her mind not on a handful of shocking words but on complicated sensations which she insists words must be able to convey, and surprising things are constantly falling into place because the poet has a remarkable gift for producing verbal equivalents of physical sensation. Reading "Cut," one feels the weird sinking hilarity which is an immediate response to any accident. Reading "Fever 103°" one can feel the marvelous superiority and euphoria of the burning. Several of the poems withheld from *Ariel* and first published in *Crossing the Water*—"Face Lift," "In Plaster," "Insomniac," "Blackberrying"—are devoted to evocations of extraordinary physical conditions; the last, which carries the poet down a hooked lane of blackberry bushes to a cliff overlooking the sea, is like a long figure for a journey through a birth canal. Her gift for evoking sound, touch, taste, as well as visual sensations, is vigorous. There is also a hardedge precision in the way Plath can present the *look* of something and its *significance* wrapped neatly together. A few quotations should illustrate these points, and incidentally to indicate her range—which is not large, but not so narrow as the commentaries enthralled by her suicide suggest. She can of course be malevolent:

> The butcher's guillotine that whispers 'How's this, how's this.'
> ["Totem"]

> Your dissatisfactions, on the other hand,
> Arrive through the mailslot with loving regularity,
> White and blank, expansive as carbon monoxide.
> ["The Rival"]

But she can also be comic; in one pleasant piece balloons are "oval soul-animals" and the toddler who bursts one "sits back, fat jug." In the bee series, when she looks inside the bee box,

> It is dark, dark,
> With the swarmy feeling of African hands
> Minute and shrunk for export . . .
> How can I let them out?
> It is the noise that appalls me most of all,
> The unintelligible syllables.
> It is like a Roman mob,
> Small, taken one by one, but my god, together! . . .
> I wonder if they would forget me
> If I just undid the locks and stood back and turned into a
>   tree.
>   ["The Arrival of the Bee Box"]

And then she can move from pure sensation, as in "Tulips":

> The tulips are too red in the first place, they hurt me.
> Even through the gift paper I could hear them breathe
> Lightly, through their white swaddlings, like an awful
>   baby . . .
> The tulips should be behind bars . . . They are opening
> Like the mouth of some great African cat . . .

to something that is on a borderline between sensation and hallucination, as at the close of "Berck-Plage" when a dull priest is

> Following the coffin on its flowery cart like a beautiful
>   woman,
> A crest of breasts, eyelids and lips
> Storming the hilltop.

And the last lines of this poem, the funereal fulfillment:

> For a minute, the sky pours into the hole like plasma.
> There is no hope, it is given up.

"Berck-Plage," incidentally, may be the most successful poem in all of Plath's late work. It has a broader scope than any other, more characters, more variety of scenery and activity, and certainly more complexity. It begins by being privately neurotic, concentrating on the author's various obsessions with sex and disease at a seaside spa, where all the other people in the landscape, and all the objects in the landscape itself, appear to threaten, sicken, and demand something of her. But unlike other lyrics which both begin and remain so, "Berck-Plage" works outward to something which is in a sense more real, one particular old man's hospital death and how the world goes on after him. This tale at once confirms, enlarges, and objectifies the poem's initial vision, and the poem gains emotional impact as it grows more "objective," since part of its point is that one is irrevocably separated from other people and can do nothing for them, until at the conclusion it has become public in the way that tragedy is public. The loss is every loss, its details sordid, the survivors helpless, the dead man's deeds "are flying off into nothing: remember us" but nobody shall remember; a ritual performs itself which is like the celebration of a wedding, and at the last moment one almost believes that a miracle of vitality may occur as the sky pours itself into the earth—but no, of course not, "it is given up." Plath's artistic development occurred so rapidly that it is easy to imagine the creation of her work as identical with the consuming of her life. A poem like "Berck-Plage" suggests that far from being at the poetic impasse her intense subjectivity implies, she was even in her last few months prepared to apply the method to matter outside of her own skin.

The method, to summarize, depends on an inability or unwillingness to perform within prior boundaries of socially and historically accepted behavior, plus a feverish craving for what Thoreau meant by "reality," plus the technical skill to represent that reality. The method is a kind of journalism of obsessions—hasty, flashy, but it works. It is a contemporary as well as a perennial American style; we find things like it in our prose, from Kerouac to Mailer, whenever a writer wants to collapse aesthetic distance and be subversive and sensational. We find things like it in painting and graphics—Rauschenberg, Warhol—whenever there is attraction-repulsion toward the slick images, at once trivial and demonic, generated by American commerce.

Some time ago while visiting China I had a conversation pertaining to Plath with an elderly Chinese woman poet who in youth had studied in the United States. She was catching up on events in American poetry subsequent to China's emergence from the Cultural Revolution. The subject was our suicides—Berryman, Plath and Sexton were mentioned—and the way suicide exemplified our culture. Why, she wondered, was Western literature in general and American literature in particular so full of mental torment and imbalance, instead of stressing, as the Chinese have done, serenity and balance? Why do we keep encouraging individualism and the cult of experience when we see that it makes people sick?

Why indeed? We in the West apparently adore individual liberty, which includes the liberty to suffer, where China adores collectivity. We have no Confucius teaching the commitment of men's intelligence to order and stability within the concentric circles of self, family, society. China has no Christ. We lack the *I Ching*. They lack the red thread of Romantic Agony. This was not a comfortable conversation for me.

It was also not a private conversation; there were journalists present, though our visit was ostensibly informal. In another city I learned that this same earnest lady had recently been attacked in the Chinese literary press for having published a series of poems too "mystical" for the mass of workers to understand, meaning that the poems had been somewhat introspective and had expressed feelings of loneliness. So there it is: Chinese today are not supposed to have the freedom to contemplate, in a poem of their own language and time, loneliness as a human possibility. We are on the other hand addicted to it though it makes us sick. I remember another poem of Emily Dickinson's, one which begins "The heart asks pleasure first" and concludes with "The liberty to die." In that nutshell rests the connection between American narcissism and American self-destructiveness. We are "free" to slide from one to the other. It is true for us that the blood jet is poetry and that there is no stopping it. Sylvia Plath's poetry is a withering into the truth of a national predicament.

NOTES

1. The acclaim, in America, begins with Robert Lowell's encomiastic introduction to the Harper and Row edition (New York, 1966), which makes the poet "hardly a person at all, or a woman, certainly not another 'poetess,' but one of those super-real, hypnotic, great classical heroines," another Sappho or Medea; through approvals like "a bitter triumph, proof of the capacity of poetry to give to reality the greater permanence of the imagination," (George Steiner, *Newsweek*, June 20, 1966); to the culmination of popularization, "one of the most marvellous volumes of poetry published for a very long time," (*Time*, June 10, 1966). The attacks tend to complain of the publicity hoopla, and to express antagonism about the type of personality, e.g., "a kind of female hardness which I find resistable," (Marius Bewley, *Hudson Review*, Oct. 1966), or the type of poetry, e.g., "Subjects are not really examined . . . they become opportunities for the personality to impose itself . . . it is best viewed as a case study," (Don Jaffe, *Saturday Review*, Oct. 15, 1966).
2. M. L. Rosenthal, *The New Poets: American and British Poetry Since World War II* (New York: Oxford University Press, 1967), p. 83.
3. Sylvia Plath, *The Collected Poems*, ed. Ted Hughes (New York: Harper & Row, 1981), pp. 295–96.

That Story

The Changes of Anne Sexton

I.

Anne Sexton is the easiest poet in the world to condescend to. Critics get in line for the pleasure of filing her under N for Narcissist and announcing that she lacks reticence. A recent example: "She indulges in self-revelation without stint, telling all in an *exposé* of her innermost workings that amounts to literary *seppuku*." The critic wonders whether "such messy preoccupations will remain to stain the linen of the culture for long or whether good taste bleaches out even the most stubborn stain eventually."[1]

In letters as in life, to expose a personal fragility is to invite attack. Cruelty and contempt follow vulnerability, just as respect follows snobbishness; it is a law of human nature. Having been on both sides of this reflex, I suspect that the sneer derives from fear—a fear of being stung into imaginative sympathy—and in Anne Sexton's case I suspect that the fear is threefold.

First of all, Sexton's material is heavily female and biological. She gives us full helpings of her breasts, her uterus, her menstruation, her abortion, her "tiny jail" of a vagina, her love life, her mother's and daughters' breasts, everyone's operations, the act of eating, the way her father's "serpent, that mocker, woke up and pressed against me / like a great god" when she danced with him after much champagne at a wedding, even the trauma of her childhood enemas. Preoccupied with the flesh, she swings between experiencing it as sacred and fertile and experiencing it as filthy and defiled. This distinguishes her from Plath, for whom the body is mainly an emblem of pain and mutilation. But the distinction will not be an interesting one to the timid reader. Far more than Plath, Sexton challenges our residual certainties that the life of the body should be private and not public, and that women especially should be seen and not heard, except among each other, talking about their messy anatomies. We believe, I think, that civilization will fall if it is otherwise.

Second, Sexton is assertively emotional. A love junkie who believes "touch" is "the kingdom and the kingdom come," she is driven by an unquenchable need for acceptance and caresses, and by bottomless guilt that she herself has been insufficiently loving to others. Simultaneously, the poetry presses intimately toward its audience. Feel what I feel, it says. Accept me, love me, love everything about me, my strength, my weakness. This of course is very much a feminine sort of demand, or rather it is a demand we discourage men from making explicitly (disguised versions are acceptable) and encourage women to make, with predictable results. Remember Marilyn Monroe? The egotistical sublime we tolerate; not the egotistical pathetic. The demand for love is narcissistic and childish. It is usually self-defeating, since most of us respond to another's need for love with aversion. Insofar as we manage (barely) to keep the upper lip stiff in our own lives, we judge neediness (in excess of our own) to be immoral. In the same way, wealth judges poverty and success perceives failure to be a consequence of low character. We understand that beggars and cripples exist, but do they have to put themselves where we can see them?

But what is most distressing about Sexton, I think, is her quality of unresignedness. She writes more fiercely than any poet in our time about physical and mental bliss and the holiness of the heart's affections. Her explorations of pathology are feverish attempts to "gnaw at the barrier" dividing us from each other and from the "weird abundance" of our creative capacities. She is sure not only that poetry saved her own life but that it can save others' lives. Many of her poems are gestures of rather pure human generosity. "To My Lover Returning to His Wife" and "December 12th" in *Love Poems* are two examples. Typically her work enacts a pitched battle between Thanatos and Eros, self-loathing and self-love, suicide and survival. This too is irritating. "The mass of men lead lives of quiet desperation," wrote Thoreau above a century ago, trying to twit them out of it. "We think of the key, each in his prison, / Thinking of the key, each confirms a prison," wrote Eliot a half-century back, on the way to his conversion to Christianity. But consider how much of our literature, our high literature especially, and most especially our high poetry, confirms the prison. We are instructed perhaps in its interior decoration, but not encouraged to seek escape. John Fowles' *Daniel Martin* muses "how all through his writing life, he had avoided the happy ending, as if it were somehow in bad taste . . . offensive, in an intellectually privileged caste, to suggest publicly that anything might turn out well." If each in his cell believes himself locked up forever, the last thing he wants to hear from a neighboring cell is the noise of scratching, poundings, screamings for the jailer.

Antipathy to a writer like Sexton makes sense if we assume that poetry must somehow be decorous. Obviously a great deal of poetry, both great and trivial, is so. But I see no real reason why poetry should be limited to tasteful confirmations of my psychic *status quo ante*, or indeed why it should be limited in any way. Reticence and good taste are excellent things, but unscrewing the doors from their jambs is a good thing too. Our original sin as humanists is a tendency to forget that nothing human is alien to any of us. This means that the crazy suicidal lady is not to be condescended to by me. It also means that she is one of the inhabitants of my own proper attic, whom I deny at my peril. A poem does not have to be, yet may legitimately be, "an axe for the frozen sea" of sympathy and self-recognition "within us," provided only that its language be living and its form just.

This brings me to the vexed question of Anne Sexton's artistry, where I must say immediately and with regret that she is not a *fine* artist. At her best she is coarse. Musically her instrument is the kazoo. If Plath, say, is porcelain and Robert Lowell bronze, Sexton is brightly painted earthenware. Reading every book of hers but *Transformations,* I burn with the desire to edit. She repeats herself without noticing. Her early poems before she hits her stride tend to be too stiff, her late ones tend to be shapeless. Her phrasing is sometimes sentimental, her endings sometimes flat.

And yet the writing dazzles. Sexton's colloquial line, vigorous, flexible and earthy, is not only a standing rebuke to every sort of false dignity but a strategy for redeeming the common life. Her organic and domestic imagery captures species of phenomena for poetry that were never there before. Her metaphors, breathtaking as ski-jumps, direct attention both to the play of language and to the writer's intelligence—which is not the same as bookishness—and sheer capacity to describe. One does not rapidly exhaust the significance of a poem about the mad that says "what large children we are" and mentions the night nurse who "walks on two erasers," or a poem about a hospital stay concluding with the lines "and run along, Anne, and run along now, / my stomach stitched up like a football / for the game." Is one's body really a toy? To others; to the self? Consider a fantasy of dying that says, "I moved like a lobster, / slower and slower," or a quick allegory of the poet's life in which Jonah, finding he cannot escape the whale, "cocked his head attentively / like a defendant at his own trial," or the simile of "tears falling down like mud," or the story of Eve giving birth to a rat "with its bellyful of dirt / and its hair seven inches long" that she did not realize was ugly. It is writerliness and nothing else that enables Sexton to re-create the child-self more keenly than Roethke, to define inner demons more clearly than Lowell, and to evoke the complicated tensile strands of intimate relationships, which include physical need and revulsion, affection and fear, pride and guilt, resentment, jealousy and admiration, better than most novelists. As to the primitive style, anyone who thinks it is easier to write "raw" than "cooked" should try it.

Often Sexton's best poems in the early books are not the harrowing accounts of private trauma which understandably most gripped her first readers, but poems where self-knowledge makes possible the verbal crystallization of some larger piece of the human condition. "Housewife," a ten-line poem with four hairpin turns and a final two lines that are as important as the first two of "The Red Wheel Barrow," is a good example. It is this that brings me to my main subject. Though Sexton is always a strong poet of the subjective self, in the middle of her career her center of gravity shifted. Beginning with *Transformations,* which was a sort of poetic self-initiation, she set the uninhibited self to work interpreting prior, external, shared cultural traditions. The texts I want to examine are *Transformations,* which is her most successful single book because of its brilliant fusion of public with personal matter; "The Jesus Papers" in *The Book of Folly,* which is her most shocking and subversive work; and the poetry of spiritual quest in *The Death Notebooks* and *The Awful Rowing Toward God,* which is her most tragic. I believe that "confessional" or not, all these poems change the way we must look at our shared past. As their themes are increasingly ambitious, their conclusions are increasingly significant culturally. Obviously they also change the way we must look at Sexton.

II.

In the winter of 1969–70, with four volumes of intimately personal poems behind her, Anne Sexton embarked on a new sort of venture. The early work dealt with the poet's family, her struggles against madness, her loves, her terrors, her desires. "That narrow diary of my mind" was laid publicly bare both as a personal necessity and in the faith that to reveal rather than conceal one's private nightmares was to perform a poetic service. The orientation of her poetry was psychoanalytic, as befitted a poet who began writing as a form of therapy following mental breakdown, who enacted in her poems the analysand's self-probing through examination of relationships with others, and who explained the vitality of her images by saying that "poetry, after all, milks the unconscious." Of all the poets subsequently labeled confessional or extremist—Snodgrass, Lowell, Berryman, Plath—she was the least reticent personally, and the most eager to have her poems "mean something to someone else." Public popularity had spectacularly confirmed Sexton's convictions. For much of 1969 the poet immersed herself with the aid of a Guggenheim grant in the autobiographical drama *Mercy Street,* a work of extreme self-saturation which played for some weeks in the fall at the American Place Theater to mixed but respectful reviews. Up until this point, Sexton had not tried "to give you something else, / something outside of myself."[2] Self was the center, self the perimeter, of her vision.

Concerning the new series of poems which retold sixteen fairy tales from the Brothers Grimm, neither the poet nor her publishers expressed great confidence. Houghton Mifflin wondered whether she should publish them at all, and wanted to consult an outside reader. Sexton was defensive and apologetic, worrying that "many of my former fans are going to be disappointed that these poems do not hover on the brink of insanity," and acknowledging that they were "a departure from my usual style . . . they lack the intensity and confessional force of my previous work." To persuade herself and her publishers that the work was good, she solicited an opinion from Stanley Kunitz. To boost it with the public, she arranged for an admiring preface by Kurt Vonnegut, Jr.

Transformations breaks the confined circle of a poetic mode Sexton had needed but outgrown, that of the purely personal. That folktales carry a heavy cultural burden has been understood since they were first collected. Mircea Eliade tells us they represent "an infinitely serious and responsible adventure" which he identifies with the universal ordeal of initiation, "passing by way of a symbolic death and resurrection from ignorance and immaturity to the spiritual age of the adult." Bruno Bettelheim believes they provide children with models for the mastery of psychological problems, teach them the necessity of struggle, and embody through fantasy "the process of healthy human development." We see these tales, in other words, as the expression of a social mandate favoring individual growth.

Sexton does not alter Grimm's plots. Her fidelity to the stories preserves what Eliade calls the "initiatory scenario," and this may partially explain why a poet who was perennially torn between remaining a child and assuming adulthood was attracted to these tales in the first place. Formally, the plot lines give her what she never had before: something nominally outside of her personal history to write about. What she does with this material is to seize it, crack it open, and *make* it personal. The result is at once a brilliant interpretation and a valid continuation of folktale tradition—and a piece of poetic subversion, whereby the "healthy" meanings we expect to enjoy are held up to icy scrutiny.

Syntax and diction in *Transformations* are conspicuously and brazenly twentieth-century American, stripped to the colloquial bone, in a mode probably generated for American poetry by Eliot's "Journey of the Magi." The technique brings us closer to the unsentimental pre-Christian origins of these stories, much as the language of Eliot's "Magi" intends not to deflate the significance of Christ's nativity but to force the reader to confront it more nakedly. But unlike Eliot (or Pound, or their imitators), far from being interested in the past for its own sake, Sexton makes the time of the tales our own. In her "Snow White and the Seven Dwarfs":

> the virgin is a lovely number:
> cheeks fragile as cigarette paper,
> arms and legs made of Limoges,
> lips like Vin du Rhône,
> rolling her china-blue doll eyes
> open and shut.

This is the opening tale and sets the tone. Of the miller's daughter in "Rumpelstiltskin," threatened with extinction if she does not spin straw into gold, the narrator condoles, "Poor thing. / To die and never see Brooklyn." In "Cinderella" the heroine

> slept on the sooty hearth each night
> and walked around looking like Al Jolson.

The reader's initial response to these anachronisms may be one of delighted shock—Cinderella and Al Jolson, yes, of course, think of the parallels—it is like a blue volt leaping a gap. We need to remember that just such modernization and adaptation, making the tales locally meaningful, is what peasants and poets have done with traditional lore for millennia. The stories would never survive without it. But Sexton's telescoping of past and present is also a surface manifestation of a more profound interpretive activity.

The poet's effort to understand her stories on her own terms precipitates a transformed view of traditional social values, particularly those associated with feminine life patterns: love and marriage, beauty, family, and most radically, the idea of goodness and moral responsibility, all of which she slices through like butter. The fairy-tale ending of marriage, supposed to represent romantic and financial security ever after, becomes, ironically, "that story"—incredible in the first place, and, were it credible, pathetically dull:

> Cinderella and the prince
> lived, they say, happily ever after,
> like two dolls in a museum case
> never bothered by diapers or dust,
> never arguing over the timing of an egg,
> never telling the same story twice,
> never getting a middle-aged spread,
> their darling smiles pasted on for eternity.
> Regular Bobbsey Twins.
> That story.

Half of Sexton's tales end in marriage, and most of these marriages are seen as some form of either selfishness or captivity. Regarding the value of beauty, we learn in "Snow White" that an innocent virgin's unconscious beauty makes her a stupid doll, a commodity, while an experienced woman's conscious beauty makes her not only cruel but doomed. "Beauty is a simple passion, / but, oh my friends, in the end / you will dance the fire dance in iron shoes." Moreover, since "a woman *is* her mother," at the wedding celebration during which the stepmother gets tortured to death in those iron shoes, Snow White chillingly begins "referring to her mirror / as women do." Describing the sacred emotion of mother-love, Sexton in "Rumplestiltskin" remarks with pure contempt:

> He was like most new babies,
> as ugly as an artichoke
> but the queen thought him a pearl.
> She gave him her dumb lactation,
> delicate, trembling, hidden,
> warm, etc.

While none of the protagonists in Sexton's versions is described in terms of his or her virtue, which is Grimm's as it should be, pre-Disney and amoral, "evil" characters and deviant behavior commonly receive her sympathy. The witch in "Hansel and Gretel" is cannibalistic and terrifying, as in the original, and her death is represented as poetic justice. But the poem's prologue has been a fantasia on the theme of a normally affectionate mother's desire to "eat up" her son, and the epilogue provocatively suggests that in a world governed by eating or being eaten, the witch in "the woe of the oven" has been a sacrifice "like something religious." Does Sexton mean that the witch is a Christ figure? Is this a reference to the subduing of the mother-goddess by a civilized daughter allied with the patriarchy? (Louise Glück's "Gretel in Darkness," by the way, raises similar questions.) In "Rapunzel," Sexton sees the witch as a lesbian in love with her imprisoned girl, and the poem stresses the emotional poignance of the older woman's loss, while perfunctorily dismissing the normality of the heterosexual lovers. "Rumplestiltskin" and other stories follow a similar pattern, prodding us toward identification with antagonist-loser instead of protagonist-winner.

By the same token a number of characters we have conventionally accepted as good are made repellent. In "The Maiden

Without Hands," the king who weds the mutilated girl is motivated by "a desire to own the maiming / so that not one of us butchers / will come to him with crowbars." So long as the queen is a cripple, the king will feel secure in his own wholeness. (This, by the way, is one of the few occasions when Sexton writes, albeit allegorically, about her own marriage. Asked in an interview whether she was not afraid of hurting others by her intimate revelations of family life, she explained that she wrote mainly about the dead who could not be hurt, and avoided saying painful things about the living.) In "The Twelve Dancing Princesses," which is tranformed to an Eros-versus-Logos, or Pleasure-Principle-versus-Superego parable, Logos unfortunately wins, in the person of the clever young man who finds out where the irresponsible princesses do their dancing. His mean-minded success brings an end to their enjoyable night life. The shocking final poem, "Briar Rose" (Sleeping Beauty), eliminates the heroine's mother and makes the father not merely the possessive maintainer of his daughter's prepubescent purity—"He forced every male in the court / to scour his tongue with Bab-o"—but its incestuous exploiter. Sleep in this poem brings "a voyage" into regressive infantilism. Wakened after her hundred-years' sleep, Briar Rose cries "Daddy! Daddy!" What she will see for the rest of her life when she wakens from the nightmares that plague her is

> another kind of prison.
> It's not the prince at all,
> but my father
> drunkenly bent over my bed,
> circling the abyss like a shark,
> my father thick upon me
> like some sleeping jellyfish.

Here and everywhere Sexton's interpretations discover and release elements already implicit in the stories. Over and over one thinks "of course." Were we to look at these poems as moral texts, we would have to see in them a demand for some transvaluation of social values.

But the appeal of the tales is primarily neither moral nor immoral. They are, as the central fact of magic in them partially indicates, rooted in and addressed to something less rational in our natures than the impulse toward social reform. Joseph Campbell makes the obvious point that folktale, like dream and myth, derives ultimately from the individual psyche, modified by the successions of cultures it travels through, and that its images are not simply relics of religious or superstitious periods in cultural history but projections of universal and primitive human desires and fears. It is proper, therefore, that Sexton's handling of these tales, while unconventionally personal and morally skeptical, is nevertheless designed to maintain, not reduce, their psychic impact. The poet does not rationalize or explain. She narrates, and with great swiftness and skill. She is funny, which makes sense since comedy is a major element in the traditional stories. She is intensely vivid. Her style excites, rather than soothes, the senses. Her imagery, to borrow a term from tabloids and horror movies, is sensational, full of food and feeding, sexuality, greed, and death—often fused, in a kind of synesthesia of appetites.

"Snow White," the first story in the volume, is sensationally and gratuitously oral. It tells us that the virgin is "unsoiled . . . white as a bonefish," and a few lines later that her stepmother has been "eaten, of course, by age." Where in Grimm the evil queen wants Snow White's heart merely as proof of her death, Sexton's stepmother expresses a cruder longing: "Bring me her heart . . . and I will salt it and eat it." Brought a boar's heart by the compassionate hunter, "the queen chewed it up like cube steak."

Proceeding with the story, Sexton embroiders. Snow White on entering the strange cottage eats "seven chicken livers" before sleeping, and then we meet what I and most of my students regard as the best single metaphor in the book, "the dwarfs, those little hot dogs." Revived after her first coma, her heroine is "as full of life as soda pop." When she bites the poison apple, the dwarfs "washed her with wine / and rubbed her with butter," though to no avail. "She lay as still as a gold piece." The passive coin, recalling Plath's "I am your jewel, I am your valuable, / The pure gold baby," parallels food in its appeal to greed.

Other poems similarly ply us with images of the tactile, the expensive, the devourable. The girl in "Rumplestiltskin" is "lovely as a grape." The dwarf commits suicide by tearing himself in two, "somewhat like a split broiler." Feeding and sexuality are cheerfully identified in the bawdy poem "The Little Peasant," tragically identified in "Rapunzel," where women in love "feed off each other." In "Little Red Riding Hood" and "Hansel and Gretel," Sexton again implies the interchangeability of feeding and being fed on, in dramas of death and rebirth.

Where the Grimm stories are violent, Sexton does not skimp on pain and gore, but describes with inventive detail:

> First your toes will smoke
> and then your heels will turn black
> and you will fry upward like a frog . . .
>
> ["Snow White"]

When Cinderella's sister cuts a toe off to fit the shoe, we see

> the blood pouring forth.
> That is the way with amputations.
> They don't just heal up like a wish

and both sisters at Cinderella's wedding have their eyes pecked out, leaving "two hollow spots . . . like soup spoons." Well over half the tales include death or mutilation, and both in the individual poems and cumulatively, Sexton's images of killing and eating in *Transformations* seem not merely childish but infantile.

That, I think, is the point. The evocation of these desires and terrors reminds us of powers we can scarcely control even as adults, in our lives and in the world. We are reminded of the helpless ur-self whose whole world is touch and taste, who fantasizes omnipotence, who dreads annihilation in a thousand ways. And it is this self, we understand when reading *Transformations,* that generates fairy tales.

III.

Although Sexton did not again write in the manner of *Transformations*, the volume marks a turning point. She had learned how to interpret the impersonal by means of the personal, the symbol belonging to a culture by experience belonging to the self. She had exercised for the first time a gift for iconoclasm regarding social and moral conventions. She had acquired, as her later work shows, a taste for the quasi-mythic narrative. Her final finished books, *The Book of Folly* (1972), *The Death Notebooks* (1974), and *The Awful Rowing Toward God* (1974), return to a predominantly autobiographical mode. But they are bolder in language, formally more experimental, and readier to challenge convention, than any of her earlier work. In them the poet increasingly sees herself not as merely a private person, certainly not as a psychoanalytic case study, but as the heroine in a spiritual quest. At the same time, the question of what it means to be feminine—not simply to the self but to the culture and within the religion created by that culture— deepens and darkens. In an early (1965) *Hudson Review* interview, Sexton says, "It's very hard to reveal yourself . . . I'm hunting for the truth . . . behind everything that happens to you, every act, there is another truth, a secret life." What the late books reveal is that behind the "live or die" struggle in Sexton's life was another struggle, which led her first to a re-envisioning of Christian myth, then to a re-imagining of God the Father. I am tempted to say that Sexton's final wrestling was between loving and loathing God, and that she lost it because she knew too much.

The Book of Folly makes us think about gender in a way that moves a step past the deflating techniques of *Transformations*. It includes a group of *persona* pieces which enable the poet to imagine the violent personalities of one-legged man, assassin, wife beater—all of them castrated figures for whom woman is enemy, all of them evidently *animus*-figures for Sexton, as are "the ambition bird" in the finely sardonic and self-critical opening poem, and the destructive doppelganger in "The Other." In "The Red Shoes," a spinoff from *Transformations*, ambition is secretly and shamefully handed down from mother to daughter, is uncontrollable, and destroys them. "Anna Who Was Mad" and "The Hex" are secular salvation and damnation poems struggling with the poet's guilty fear that her ongoing life is responsible for the madness and death of the beloved aunt whose namesake she is. In "Mother and Daughter" Sexton's tone is glad and proud as she relinquishes "my booty, my spoils, my Mother & Co." and celebrates the daughter's growth to womanhood, but what womanhood means is:

> carrying keepsakes to the boys,
> carrying powders to the boys,
> carrying, my Linda, blood to
> the bloodletter.

There is a figure in the carpet here.[3] In all these poems self-sacrifice is the condition of self-acceptance, and to be feminine is to be either powerless or punished. The "Angels of the Love Affair" sonnet sequence, inspired by Rilke, challenges a set of elemental angels to know and exorcise what the poet knows of shame, defilement, paralysis, despair and solitude. In the one poem where the poet remembers herself taking a pleasurable initiative (stealing grandfather's forbidden raspberries), the angel is a punitive lady "of blizzards and blackouts." The three prose narratives in *The Book of Folly* still more clearly identify passive feminine roles (daughter, wife, erotic object) with victimization and self-victimization. The one figure who seems to escape passivity, the protagonist's adventurous friend Ruth in "The Letting Down of the Hair," finally finds Christ—and kills herself. Sexton does not tell us why. But the series of seven short poems entitled "The Jesus Papers" may explain.

Prior to *The Book of Folly*, in occasional poems dealing with Christ, Sexton had evidently identified with him as sufferer and public performer. "When I was Christ, I felt like Christ," she said of "In the Deep Museum." "My arms hurt, I desperately wanted to pull them in off the Cross. When I was taken down off the Cross, and buried alive, I sought solutions; I hoped they were Christian solutions." "That ragged Christ, that sufferer, performed the greatest act of confession." In "The Exorcists," an early poem about abortion, the title implies ironically that an aborted fetus is being cast out like a demon, but the poem's text, with its "I know you not" refrain, implies that on the contrary it is a Christ whom the speaker is betraying. Many of Sexton's letters depict an intense need for faith undermined by solid skepticism: "In case it's true, I tell my Catholic friend . . . in case it's true, I tell myself, and plead with it to be true after all. No matter what I write, I plead with it to be true!" (*Letters*, p. 125).[4] "God? spend half time wooing R. Catholics who will pray *for* you in case it's true. Spend other half knowing there is certainly no god. Spend fantasy time thinking that there is a life after death, because surely my parents, for instance, are not dead, they are, good god!, just buried" (*Letters*, p. 235). "Oh, I really believe in God—it's Christ that boggles the mind" (*Letters*, p. 346). "Yes, it is time to think about Christ again. I keep putting it off. If he is the God/ man, I would feel a hell of a lot better. If there is a God . . . how do you explain him swallowing all those people up in Pakistan? Of course there's a God, but what kind is he?" (*Letters*, pp. 368–69). Sexton also experienced visions, of varied duration and of great physical urgency, of Christ, Mary, God, the martyred saints, the devil, in which "I feel that I can touch them almost . . . that they are part of me . . . I believed that I was talking to Mary, that her lips were upon my lips," she said in an interview. None of this data, however, explains the radical vision of "The Jesus Papers," which is a systematic and structured—if miniature—reinterpretation of Christian myth, as *Transformations* is of Grimm. The subject is of course far more audacious; indeed, only two other poets in English have attempted it, Milton in *Paradise Regained* and Blake in *The Everlasting Gospel*. Was Jesus a man? Very well then, let the poet imagine what manner of man. Let her begin, since much Christian iconography dwells on his infancy, by imagining what manner of infant, and take it from there. Allowing for the vast difference in scale, Sexton's Jesus is as disagreeable as Milton's in *Paradise Regained*—and perhaps as unintentionally so.

The opening poem, "Jesus Suckles," consists of three sections of dwindling length. As so often in Sexton we are in the mind of someone utterly dependent on love. The language at first is erotic-playful, rich, organic, unstructured—one of Sexton's catalogs in which the condition of happiness is expressed through images of fertility. There is a tone of amplified gratification, rather like that of "In Celebration of My Uterus," and for the same reason. It is the mental effect of physical bliss:

> Mary, your great
> white apples make me glad . . .
> I'm a jelly-baby and you're my wife.
> You're a rock and I the fringy algae.
> You're a lily and I'm the bee that gets inside . . .
> I'm a kid in a rowboat and you're the sea,
> the salt, you're every fish of importance.

But then:

> No. No.
> All lies.
> I am small
> and you hold me.
> You give me milk
> and we are the same
> and I am glad.
>
> No. No.
> All lies.
> I am a truck. I run everything.
> I own you.

First metaphor is killed, then the love, joy and sense of universal connection that generated the metaphor. We have a tidy drama of pleasure-principle succumbing to reality-principle, with both natural and supernatural implications. The poem reminds us that to a god, or a boy child, grateful love and helplessness are "all lies," and that reality—assuming the dualistic universe that Christianity does assume—means power, repugnance toward the flesh, and rejection of the mother. The relevant Biblical text attributes this moment of brutality to

Jesus' adolescence: "Woman, what have I to do with thee?" Sexton merely pushes the time back. Blake's "To Tirzah" is a comparably cruel poem on the same text. The initial imagery implies that Mary is Mother Nature, or the pre-Christian goddesses who represent her divine fertility. Man and God are her privileged superiors and historical conquerors. The modern technological outcome of the split between Flesh and Logos which Christianity sacralizes is modestly accommodated by the synecdoche "truck."[5]

The succeeding poems trace what follows from the initial willed division of Jesus from Mary, boy child from mother, the will to control from the willingness to fondle and nurture. While the rest of the human and animal kingdom frolics and propagates, Jesus fasts. "His penis no longer arched with sorrow over Him"—the rainbow image recalling God's forgiving covenant with Noah and mankind—but "was sewn onto Him like a medal," an outrageous metaphor that not only disparages Jesus' celibacy but calls into question that Christian replacement of sexual love by *caritas*. Though he still desires Mary when asleep, he subdues his need, uses his penis as a chisel à la Rodin, and produces a Pietà so that they will be united in his death. *Civilization and Its Discontents* is the necessary gloss for this poem. For the next one *Justine* might do. When Jesus encounters the harlot Mary Magdalen being stoned ("Stones came at her like bees to candy / and sweet redheaded harlot that she was / she screamed out *I never, I never*"), he raises her up and efficiently heals her "terrible sickness" then and there by lancing with his thumbs her breasts, "those two boils of whoredom," until the milk runs out. Sexton's deadpan combination of Biblical and contemporary language here is typical:

> The harlot followed Jesus around like a puppy
> for He had raised her up.
> Now she forsook her fornications
> and became His pet.

In "Jesus Cooks" and "Jesus Summons Forth" we get the miracle of the loaves and fishes as a sleight of hand act and the raising of Lazarus by assembling his bones as if he were a model airplane kit. "Tenderness" appears in a single line and appears to be part of the instructions. As with the poems on Jesus' sexuality, the poet's wry self-projection is important here. The roles of food-provider and healer were Sexton's, as was the role of public performer for whom feeling was part of the act. In the bitterly comic "Jesus Dies," the crucifixion is like an ultimate Sexton poetry reading, where Jesus' self-revelation of his sore need for God—a "man-to-man thing" that is half-competitive, half-desperate—is mingled with furious irritation at his audience's sensation-seeking.

From crucifixion Sexton does not move on to resurrection, but drops back to another woman-poem, "Jesus Unborn," which turns out to be, like "Jesus Suckles," a judgment of the Virgin's role in Christianity. It is the moment before the Annunciation, and again the imagery is lushly natural. Mary sits among olive trees, feels lethargic as an animal, wants to settle down like a camel or doze like a dog:

> Instead a strange being leans over her
> and lifts her chin firmly
> and gazes at her with executioner's eyes.

So much for how many centuries of Mariolatry? how many centuries of sacred iconography? But in case Sexton has not made herself clear, she appends to "The Jesus Papers" a final poem entitled "The Author of the Jesus Papers Speaks," which defines the place not only of Mary but of all womankind in Western religion. It is a dream-poem in three tiny episodes. First, Sexton milks a great cow, but instead of "the moon juice, the white mother," blood spurts "and covered me with shame." Several related readings are possible here: blood may be menstrual blood, shameful because taboo, sign of female pollutedness; or blood as sign that mothers surrender their own lives for others' lives, like beasts; or a reminder that all life leads to death. The cow might be Nature, or Mother-goddess, or Sexton's own mother who shamed and blamed her and whose "double image" she was. We have the beginnings of a rich female drama but there is no development, for at this point God speaks to Sexton and says, "People say only good things about Christmas. If they want to say something bad,/they whisper."

This is a change in tone as well as a non sequitur, it is funny, and it gives us a God who, like a boss or an earthly father, is half-uncomfortable with the way his governing role divides him from those he governs. God seems to be interrupting a mother-daughter interview, making a bid for attention—and sympathy—for his own concerns. But why should anyone say bad things about Christmas? Is God paranoid? Or guilty? Or, if this dream is taking place in the twentieth century, might we say that He doesn't know the half of it? In any case, Sexton's response is to go to the well and draw a baby out, which in her own drama means she moves from daughter-role to mother-role, and in God's terms means she produces the Christ. Judging by the poem's final seven lines, this is the submissive gesture God was looking for.

> Then God spoke to me and said:
> Here. Take this gingerbread lady
> and put her in your oven.
> When the cow gives blood
> and the Christ is born
> we must all eat sacrifices.
> We must all eat beautiful women.

Now the changed tone tells us that God has been, as it were, reassured and confirmed in His Godliness by Sexton's feminine compliance, much as a man tired and complaining after work will have his dignity renewed by a wife or daughter laying out a perfect dinner. This final speech is authoritative not only in the sense of issuing commands but in the sense of assuming verbal command over the poem's prior structure of symbols. Nature and femaleness (cow, moon, milk, blood), at first large and powerful, are reduced to domesticity and powerlessness. Dream-cow becomes cookie. "We" must at the advent of Christianity not *make* sacrifices but eat them, and God's pseudo-cosy "we" is the velvet glove of paternal imperative. The substitution of gingerbread lady for the bread that is Christ's body reminds us that the Christ-cult (and the Passover feast it builds on) takes its symbolism from earlier Middle Eastern religions in which the object of primary worship was the fertile and nourishing mother. Perhaps it implies that the misogyny of the Church and its need to subordinate ("sacrifice") women derive ultimately from a forgotten time of usurpation and a dread lest the "cow" move again to the forefront of our dream.

As a comment on the "Jesus papers" sequence, the epilogue is a recapitulation of the theme of divine male power and mortal female submission. But it also fixes the position of its author as one who is by no means protesting the images of herself and other women within Christianity. On the contrary, she complies, she obeys, in this final dream, just as Mary and the harlot comply within the sequence. For herself, and on behalf of all beautiful women, she accepts humiliation. We may even say, since after all the dream is her invention, that she requires it.

IV.

I need some such explanation to understand Sexton's religious poetry in *The Death Notebooks* and *The Awful Rowing Toward God*. For in these books, like a defeated athlete, she hurls herself again and again into a contest that her own poetry should have showed her she could not win, trying to imagine—trying to experience—a God she could both believe in and be loved by. The decisive intelligence which dismantles religious myth is no match for the child-woman's ferocious need for cosmic love, and so what we see in the last two books is a poet attempting to give imaginative birth to an adequate Godhead. But since her need is no match for her doubt, what we see is heroic failure. Or rather, perhaps, her need is no match for her sense of the significance of divine power, which is the power of the parent writ very large.

The Death Notebooks begins with a seriocomic quest poem,

one of Sexton's funniest and best. It also contains the "Furies" series; the cycle of "Psalms" written in the manner of Christopher Smart, who becomes her imaginary twin and ally; and two semisurreal figures for the omnipresent Thanatos and the frustrated Eros of the poet's soul: the icy "death baby" and the despairing yet smart-aleck "Ms. Dog." *The Awful Rowing* is a series of quest poems written at breakneck speed "in a frenzy of despair and hope" shortly after her divorce in November 1973, and scarcely revised. "I cannot walk an inch / without trying to walk to God. / I cannot move a finger / without trying to reach God" is the burden of these poems. Both books are attempts to locate the self in a context of the objectively sacred, but with Sexton implicitly insisting that the realm of the sacred must answer to her private experience of reality, that the objective and subjective must be one, as she was able to make them one in *Transformations*. She is once again working through a prior tradition (God is no post-Tillich moral abstraction but an omnipotent male person), but now as if her life depended on it. Poems like "Civil War" and "Frenzy" imply, in fact, that only by an unremitting effort to create a God coextensive with her own imagination can the poet hope to be saved. This is strenuously antinomian religion, an American specialty, and a risky business in any case, riskier when the worshipper's ego is as frail as Sexton's.

"Let there be a God as large as a sunlamp to laugh his heat at you," begins the "First Psalm" of "O Ye Tongues." She prays in the course of the Psalms "that God will digest me," and at the end declares "for God was as large as a sunlamp and laughed his heat at us (i.e., Anne and Christopher) and therefore we did not cringe at the death hole." Sexton wants to imagine God as simultaneously transcendent and immanent within all flesh. He is a jigsaw with thousands of pieces, "dressed up" like a whore, an old man, a naked child, present within all domestic routines and especially present within human sexuality:

> When they fuck they are God.
> When they break away they are God.
> When they snore they are God.

In the morning they butter the toast.
They don't say much.
They are still God.

Such a God is necessarily benevolent. The sustaining of even a small faith will bring him into one's hands the way a dime used to bring forth a Coke. He has no body but wishes he had one, envying humans their bodies as we envy him his soul. If Sexton can reach him he will remove and embrace the "gnawing pestilential rat" which is her figure for her sense of inner vileness. On good days he gives milk (cf. the cow in "Jesus Papers" and *Isaiah* 66:12) and she has the pail. Salvation depends on her ability to keep "typing out the God / my typewriter believes in. / Very quick. Very intense, / like a wolf at a live heart. / Not lazy" ("Frenzy").

Sexton is full of startlingly "right" modern analogues for traditional images in Christian writing. Her lifelong rowing against the wind is the emotional equivalent of the journey in *Pilgrim's Progress*. Her "sunlamp" God emits an eerie charge that the word "sun" no longer has in our language. Her infinitely multiple jigsaw or typewriter God is oddly like Milton's figure in *Areopagitica* of the scattered body of Truth, whose form all true men must be engaged in gathering up limb by limb throughout human history, until the Second Coming "shall bring together every joint and member." Almost every poem has something like this.

What defeats Sexton is in part a sense of her own evil, the "rat" or "bowel movement" her mother tried to force out of her child-self but that still fills her to the fingertips. Hers is not a conventional sin divisible from her bodily being, and priests are unable to shrive or even comprehend it. In the long sequence of faith-doubt poems beginning with "The Dead Heart" and ending with "Is It True?," a mocking self-disgust is inextricably mingled with God's unbearable departure. The tone strongly resembles that of Hopkins in the Terrible Sonnets, and Sexton's habitual oral imagery touches close on Hopkins' "I am gall, I am heartburn. God's most deep decree / Bitter would have me taste; my taste was me." There are hints that the problem is insoluble because Sexton cannot or will not deny her identification with the flesh that divides her from God:

> We are all earthworms
> digging into our wrinkles.
> We live beneath the ground
> and if Christ should come in the form of a plow
> and dig a furrow and push us up into the day
> we earthworms would be blinded by the sudden light
> and writhe in our distress.
> As I write this sentence I too writhe.

Logically, theologically, it is inconsistent to imagine a God immanent in all bodies and a body unable to tolerate God's blinding presence. But immanence in Western religion is a heresy, and for the image of God as blinding glory there are precedents going back at least to Dante, while Christ with his plow is one of the most forceful images of Revelation. What I earlier called an "adequate" God—one powerful enough to love and accept Sexton and all of us ratlike "cursed ones falling out after"—must also be powerful enough to reject and annihilate. It is such a God, closer to Scripture than Sexton's hopeful fantasies desire, who dominates *The Awful Rowing*. Through most of the volume the tone is frenzied and agonized. God is distant, indifferent. Near the close, God is "surgical andiron." In the penultimate poem, when the poet trembles to utter her faith that God is in all matter, "heaven smashes my words."

The final poem of *The Awful Rowing* was, I think, intended to be a happy ending. When the poet finally arrives at her island, God challenges her to a game of poker. She thinks she wins because she holds a royal straight flush. God wins because he holds five aces. Here is the end of the poem and the book:

> As He plunks down His five aces
> and I sit grinning at my royal flush,
> He starts to laugh,
> the laughter rolling like a hoop out of His mouth
> and into mine,

and such laughter that He doubles right over me
laughing a Rejoice-Chorus at our two triumphs.
Then I laugh, the fishy dock laughs
the sea laughs. The Island laughs.
The Absurd laughs.

Dearest dealer,
I with my royal straight flush,
love you so for your wild card,
that untamable, eternal gut-driven *ha-ha*
and lucky love.

To my ear there is something appalling in such an ending.
Is the "lucky love" of that dreadfully lame last line supposed
to be the wild card God triumphs with? What I hear sounds
like a grotesque attempt to placate and conciliate a God of
our Fathers who is being experienced as atrocious, brutal, a
betrayer.

"Out of His mouth / and into mine . . . He doubles over
me." Is God conceivably a rapist? This power-figure, who also
inhabits the last poem of "The Jesus Papers" and the last poem
of "The Death Notebooks": is he also the father-lover of the
last poem in *Transformations*? John Donne too wanted to be
raped by God; yet "Batter my heart" and "The Rowing End-
eth," comparable in their yearning for divine union expressed
in this shared metaphor, are utterly different in emotional
resonance. Reading Donne, I am able to believe the paradox of
Christian surrender: "for I / except you enthrall me, never
shall be free, / Nor ever chaste except you ravish me." Perhaps
the reason there are so many excellent devotional writers who
are men, so few who are women, is that the feminine experi-
ence of submission is for a man a rounding-out of his usual
personality, hence truly a fulfillment and kind of freedom.
"Absolute sovereignty is what I love to ascribe to God,"
Jonathan Edwards announces, and convinces us that this is
"not only a conviction, but a delightful conviction." For a wom-
an it merely reinforces her usual social role.

On October 14, 1974, after reading galleys of *The Awful
Rowing*, Sexton killed herself. In the same year, Mary Daly

published *Beyond God the Father,* an attack on patriarchal religion. Among feminist theologians and historians of ideas it has subsequently become a commonplace assumption that the passive-female imagery of Western religion is inadequate for women's spiritual needs, and a countercultural women's search for goddess figures has become something of a cultural brushfire in England and France as well as America. Sexton has no part in that search. She is not a protest poet. Her religion is determinedly partriarchal. Her God is not Self but Other.

There is a precedent for Sexton's painful ambivalence in this matter of God the Father. Emily Dickinson, a poet aesthetically poles removed from Sexton, seems also to have modeled her God on the image of a father. One of her roles with him is that of coy little girl, a pose that makes modern audiences twitch. But girlishness was an approved tone in Dickinson's own time, especially for unmarried women, as we know by its ubiquitous titter in many of her letters. (There is a similar aggravated girlishness in Plath's letters to her mother.) Behind anything so ostentatiously agreeable, we feel, something disagreeable must lurk. Dickinson's portrait of God, when she does not draw him flatteringly as nice daddy, is, like Sexton's, the portrait of an indifferent brute ("Of course I cried! And did God care?"), a bully, an "Inquisitor" who may or may not grant one "the liberty to die," a foe whom one must love because defiance is impossible. "Burglar! Banker—Father!" is only the most famous of her tense portrayals. And like Sexton, Dickinson seems genuinely to have adored and needed this divine antagonist. Ancestress of rebels, she is none herself. At times it is difficult to distinguish Lord from Lover in both poets. Sexton's "rowing" figure itself has an antecedent, coincidentally or not, in Dickinson's most erotic poem, addressed to an unknown love:

> Wild Nights—Wild Nights!
> Were I with thee
> Wild nights should be
> Our luxury!

Futile—the winds—
to a Heart in port—
Done with the Compass—
Done with the Chart!

Rowing in Eden—
Ah, the Sea!
Might I but moor—Tonight—
In Thee!

The range, the demands and the risks of Sexton's poetry increased throughout her lifetime. If she failed to achieve "a Heart in port," she was not alone in that.

NOTES

1. Rosemary Johnson, "The Woman of Private (But Published) Hungers," *Parnassus* (Fall/Winter 1979):92.
2. The early volumes, all published by Houghton Mifflin, are *To Bedlam and Part Way Back* (1960), in which the apologia-poem "For John, Who Begs me Not to Enquire Further" appears; *All My Pretty Ones* (1962), *Live or Die* (1966), for which she received the Pulitzer Prize, and *Love Poems* (1969). Sexton's *Collected Poems,* with an excellent introduction by Maxine Kumin, was published by Houghton Mifflin in 1981. The interviews I quote are in J. D. McClatchy, ed., *Anne Sexton: the Artist and Her Critics* (Bloomington: Indiana University Press, 1978).
3. I mention this, I must confess, in specific irritation with W. H. Pritchard's authoritative pronouncement that "there is no figure in the poetry's carpet to worry about discovering—it's all smack on the surface," and that the late Sexton jettisoned "whatever modest technical accomplishment she possessed in favor of getting down the excitingly grotesque meanings" ("The Anne Sexton Show," *Hudson Review* 31, no. 2 [Summer 1978]:389, 391). He does not specify *what* meanings. But we do not see what we do not look for.
4. Sexton's letters are collected in *Anne Sexton: a Self-Portrait in Letters,* ed. Linda Gray Sexton and Lois Ames (Boston: Houghton Mifflin, 1977).
5. This image appears also in "Those Times . . ." of *Live or Die,* where

Sexton writes of childhood humiliations inflicted by her mother and says "I did not know that my life, in the end, / would run over my mother's like a truck." The distance between earlier and later poems makes a good index of Sexton's development. The earlier poem is private and familial; the later one locates the private scenario within a mythic context. The earlier poem is strictly autobiographical and describes the self as passive; in the later, "Jesus" becomes, among other things, a figure for active and aggressive (i.e., "male") elements in her character which she was reluctant to acknowledge while writing as a woman.

May Swenson and the Shapes of Speculation

Most humanists show very little curiosity about the physical world outside the self, and usually a positive antipathy to the mental processes we call scientific. This was not always the case. Although Western literature has only one *De Rerum Natura*, persons of letters were once expected to take all knowledge as their province, and to interpret scientific understanding as part of a unified vision of the world. Despite the expanding post-Renaissance hostility between science and art, even as late as the nineteenth century, Blake was defining the implications of Newtonian mechanics for the human imagination, and apparently anticipating aspects of post-Newtonian physics, as he anticipated so much else. Shelley was thrilled by discoveries in electricity and magnetism. Tennyson registered the seismic shock of *The Origin of Species.* When William Carlos Williams in *Paterson* makes Madame Curie's discovery of radium a major metaphor for all artistic discovery, he bridges the supposed "two cultures" completely. Science will not go away because poets ignore it, and in fact we ignore any great human enterprise at our peril. "The world," wrote Sir Francis Bacon, "is not to be narrowed till it will go into the understanding, but the understanding is to be expanded and opened till it can take in the image of the world." For practical as well as philosophical reasons, this is at least as true in the twentieth as in the seventeenth century. Yet few poets presently venture beyond dread or annoyance toward the works and ways of physics, chemistry, biology, and fewer bring back more than a gimcrack souvenir or two. The Bomb and a fuzzy idea of Relativity were popular awhile ago. Moon-landings and Ecology more recently cornered the market. What is lacking is not just information but a way of thinking.

May Swenson, born in Utah in 1919, New Yorker by adoption since 1949, has written well-received books of poems beginning with *Another Animal* in 1954 and culminating, so far, with *New & Selected Things Taking Place* in 1978.[1] She is known as a nature poet, "one of the few good poets who write good poems about nature . . . not just comparing it to states of mind or society," as Elizabeth Bishop once remarked.[2] You could cull a bestiary from her work which would include geese, turtles, an owl and its prey, another owl and its mate heard calling to each other while the poet is camping—besides a bird-watcher's multitude of bird species, a bee and a rose, frogs, fireflies, cats and caterpillars, at least one lion, one chained dog encountered daily from fierce puppyhood to "old and fat and dirty" decline, and many horses. She writes of sun, moon, clouds, landscapes and cityscapes, and always with a wondering, curious eye, an intense concern about the structure and texture of her subject, an extraordinary tactility. "The pines, aggressive as erect tails of cats," begins a poem called "Forest." Another called "Spring Uncovered" begins, "Gone the scab of ice that kept it snug, / the lake is naked," and ends where "a grackle, fat as burgundy, / gurgles on a limb" with "bottle-glossy feathers."

But beyond the naturalist's patient observation lies something else. What critics have called Swenson's "calculated naivete" or her ability to become "a child, but a highly sophisticated child,"[3] is actually that childlike ability to envision something freshly, to ask incessant questions and always be prepared for unexpected answers, required of the creative scientist. Thus she has a habit of writing poems in the form of riddles or quasi-riddles, thoroughly examining a thing while withholding its name. These are fun, first of all, and some of her nicest work rides on the fun; see, for example, "At Breakfast," which is surely the best poem anybody has ever written about the egg. At the same time, the riddle-poem captures the way an experimental mind must look at any natural phenomena, and playfully nudges us away from our dull routine of thinking that when we have named a thing we understand it. "How things really are we should like to know," she murmurs, and what else is the motive of the speculative intellect? Swenson's poetry asks as many questions as a four-year-old, she lets her questions carry her to further questions, and she wants to know not only how things are made and what they resemble, but where they are going and how we fit in.

The opening poem of *To Mix With Time* unblushingly titles itself "The Universe." *Iconographs* has poems on, for example, the response of a snail to tide, the rotation of a mobile, electronic sound, anti-matter, a telephoto of Earth taken from Orbiter 5, the history of astronomy, man as mammal and (maybe) anima, and the declaration that "THE DNA MOLE-CULE/is The Nude Descending a Staircase/a circular one." In "Let Us Prepare," the poet seriously considers the possibility of evolution "beyond the organic," although in a poem about flight—from the thistle seed to flying mammals to Lindbergh to John Glenn—she begins and concludes that "earth will not let go our foot"; thus demonstrating that she can, as a good scientist should, speculate on both sides of a given hypothesis. In "Out of My Head" she begins by making cheerfully clear that the division of subjective self from objective world is a nonproblem, and goes on to decide that since she came here in her head, "the idea is to make a vehicle/out/of it." "Almanac" takes note that between the rising and setting of a "moon"—a bruise on her fingernail:

> an unmanned airship
> dived 200 miles to the hem of space, and
> vanished. At the place of Pharaoh Cheops'
> tomb (my full moon floating yellow)
> a boat for ferrying souls to the sun
> was disclosed in a room sealed 5000 years.
>
> Reaching whiteness, this moon-speck waned

while an April rained. Across the street,
a vine crept over brick up 14 feet. And
Einstein (who said there is no hitching
post in the universe) at 77 turned ghost.

Process and connection concern her in the deepest ways:

The stone is milked to feed the tree;
the log is killed when the flame is hungry.
To arise in the other's body?

But curiosity is a habit of mind at all times. In "Welcome
Aboard the Turbojet Electra":

Why do they say 31,000 feet? Why
not yards or miles? Why four
cigarettes and no match?

There is also a fair amount of laughter at folly, often the folly
of mistaking names for things. For examples of this, applied to
diverse subjects, see "God," which is a sort of thumbnail synop-
sis of theology (or is it metaphysics?) from the pre-Socratics
through Descartes to us; and "Going to the Whitney and Walk-
ing on the Floor," which is high comedy about false and true
aesthetics.

If this is not typical women's poetry, Swenson is not a typical
woman. Ordinarily she does not write on themes that have
come to be considered feminist, although she does grapple
with them occasionally, with electrifying results. I will look at
one of those poems below. Most often, she blends, she bal-
ances. Science, technology, the mental life of observation,
speculation: she has invaded these traditionally "masculine"
territories. Yet her consistent intimacy with her world, which
contains no trace of the archetypal "masculine" will to conquer
or control it, seems archetypally "feminine." So does the way
she lets herself be precise yet tentative and vulnerable about
her observations where a comparable male poet, perhaps driv-

en by the need to overcome alienation, might be pretentious (Snyder?), pedantic (Olsen?), anxious (Ammons?) or agonized (Kinnell?); and her affinity for the small-scale object, like Emily Dickinson's, also reads like a feminine characteristic.

Readers of contemporary American women's poetry will have noticed the extraordinary richness with which it dwells on the flesh, the body, to a degree unduplicated in most men's poetry. (Check your nearest anthology if you doubt this.) To Swenson, everything in the world speaks body-language: a tree has a toenail, spring grass grows "out of each pore . . . itching," a snowplow sucks "celestial clods into its turning neck." The same poet asks, "Body my house / my horse my hound / what will I do / when you are fallen," and concludes a poem on the senses, "in the legs' lair, / carnivora of Touch." The poems associated with her mother's death ("Nature" and "That the Soul May Wax Plump") are furiously and palpatingly physical. "Poet to Tiger," a rough-and-tumble love poem which resembles no other I can think of but Gertrude Stein's "Lifting Belly," is full of the funny things people do with their bodies. When Swenson imagines her soul escaping her own body in "Ending," it is perforce through her toe, and she can't help imagining the soul's transparence as "his little jelly belly."

Is it her familiarity with, and apparent liking for, her personal fleshliness, that generates Swenson's characteristic fondness for the world's body? Or is it the other way around? If anatomy is destiny, Swenson is at home (and humorous) with that, knowing we share that fate, finding no discrepancy whatever between what some would call a woman's body and a man's mind.

But poetic originality shows itself most obviously through an original form, some shape of a poem that we have not seen, some refreshing play of syntax, a new way words have been thrown in the air and fallen together, been lain one next to the other. Exploratory poetry invites—demands—exploratory forms. When entering new territory, form can become quite palpably "an extension of content," a ship's prow, an arm reaching, a dog's nose sniffing the air.

Swenson has always had an individual style, though bearing traces here and there of Emily Dickinson, E. E. Cummings, and especially Marianne Moore. "The poet watches life with affection" could be said as aptly of her as Marianne Moore said of herself, though Swenson allows herself more relaxation, less self-protection in her watchfulness. Moore's lovely saying about inspiration and technique, "Ecstasy affords the occasion, and expediency determines the form," sounds true for Swenson too. Like Moore, and like Gertrude Stein before that, Swenson has always been committed to formal experimentation, and she has often played with the shapes of poems. I would like to dwell here on one book, *Iconographs*, in which the composition of shaped poems is systematic.

Originally published in 1970, *Iconographs* is quintessentially inventive Swenson. For reasons unexplained in the text of *Things Taking Place*, many of these poems have been visually normalized; I hope a future edition will restore their originality.

Iconographs consists of forty-six poems, each of which plays a typographical game. Each has been given a unique shape or frame. Verticals, angles and curves, quirky spacings and capitalizations have all been used. The intention, Swenson suggests in a note, has been "to cause an instant object-to-eye encounter with each poem even before it is read word-for-word. To have simultaneity as well as sequence. To make an existence in space, as well as time, for the poem." The title, she further remarks, can imply: *icon* "a symbol hardly distinguished from the object symbolized"; *icono-* from the Greek eikonos meaning "image" or "likeness"; *graph* "diagram" or "system of connections or interrelations"; *-graph* from the Greek graphe meaning "carve" . . . "indicating the instrument as well as the written product of the instrument." But such descriptions scarcely prepare us for the power of the opening poem, "Bleeding."

It would be difficult, among feminist documents, to find a stronger statement about the connection between *bleeding* and *feeling*, which in our culture are both believed to be natural to women, and a bit disgusting, and certainly threatening, while a

Bleeding

Stop bleeding   said the knife.
I would if I   could said the cut.
Stop bleeding   you make me messy with this blood.
I'm sorry said the cut.
Stop or   I will sink in farther said the knife.
Don't said the cut.
The   knife did not say it couldn't help it but
it   sank in farther.
If   only you didn't bleed said the knife I wouldn't
have   to do this.
I know   said the cut I bleed too easily I hate
that I   can't help it I wish I were a knife like
you and   didn't have to bleed.
Well   meanwhile stop bleeding will you said the knife.
Yes you   are a mess and sinking in deeper said the cut I
will have   to stop.
Have you   stopped by now said the knife.
I've almost   stopped I think.
Why must you   bleed in the first place said the knife.
For the same   reason maybe that you must do what you
must do said   the cut.
I can't stand   bleeding said the knife and sank in farther.
I hate it too said   the cut I know it isn't you it's
me you're lucky to be   a knife you ought to be glad about that.
Too many cuts around   said the knife they're
messy I don't know how   they stand themselves.
They don't said the cut.
You're bleeding again.
No I've stopped said the cut   see you are coming out now the
blood is drying it will rub   off you'll be shiny again and clean.
If only cuts wouldn't bleed   so much said the knife coming
out a little.
But then knives might become   dull said the cut.
Aren't you still bleeding a   little said the knife.
I hope not said the cut.
I feel you are just a little.
Maybe just a little but I can   stop now.
I feel a little wetness still   said the knife sinking in a
little but then coming out a   little.
Just a little maybe just enough said the cut.
That's enough now stop now do   you   feel better now said the knife.
I feel I have to bleed to   feel I   think said the cut.
I don't I don't' have to   feel said   the knife drying now
becoming shiny.

dry superiority to feeling is a major sign of desirable masculinity. And Swenson's methods are purely poetic: the low-key "said" throughout the dialogue indicating a habitual everyday encounter; the obsessively locked-in repeating of the key terms "bleeding," "bleed," "cut" and "blood"; the sound-pattern intensifying "bleed," "easily," "meanwhile"; the sound-effect of "messy" and "wetness" opposed to the hard sounds of "knife," "drying," "shiny." What the cut "feels," of course, is self-loathing. It agrees with the knife, accepts the values implicit in the terms "messy" versus "shiny." It hates its own messiness, wishes it were a knife. And of course it feels empathy for the knife, which the knife of course does not reciprocate. Yet beyond the language, the most frightening thing in the poem is that visible slash down the page, that speaks, that takes the breath away.

Why, when the knife complains of messiness, cannot the cut cry out, "I am bleeding and messy because you are cutting me, you bastard," instead of saying "I'm sorry?" Must we ourselves identify feeling with bleeding? Is the knife unable to feel, or merely unwilling? The poem does not tell. We notice only that at its conclusion, after the back-and-forth, after the pauses, the ragged streak which lacerates the text has begun to branch out.

By its sharply enclosed form, "Bleeding" epitomizes vast quantities of writing by and about women, from the masochist thrills of *The Story of O* and its ilk, to the sexual-political anguish of Marge Piercy or Robin Morgan, as well as the large and dreary intermediate terrain of poems and novels about crude and boorish male lovers. Yet—a most important further value—it makes no explicit mention of sex or of sexual roles. It does not exclude the possibility that men may be "cuts" (indeed, it recalls Shylock's moving "If you cut me, do I not bleed" and his cringing masochistic role throughout *The Merchant of Venice*) and that women may be "knives." Not persons or personalities, but a universal form of sickness has been explored here, has been stated as pattern, as coolly rendered as if the subject were the relation between a microbe and its host.

At an opposite extreme from this sort of pattern-finding, a poem called "Feel Me" takes a single induplicable event in the poet's life, and focuses on its most unique or "accidental" element. The mystery is the meaning of a father's deathbed words.

Williams suggested, as a formula for the poetic process, "in the particular to discover the universal." This poem stands as a major enactment of that idea. It is especially touching that the naturalist's habits of patient attention, and the scientific imperative of hypothesizing as many explanations as possible for any mystery, ready to accept each, yet fixing on none, have been applied so perfectly to the depths of the human condition.

Much of the power here, as well as the intelligence, derives from a cross-cut play of rhyming sounds and assonances, either reinforcing or counterpointing meaning. The first stanza alone has "right" and "not quite," "said" and "bed," "all" and "wall," "key" and "me," and finally "how did it / fit?" Later come "dying" and "trying," "worms" and the deflating "terms," "sense" and "dense," "emulate" and "state," the pathos of "first" followed by "burst," "feeling" and "kneeling," "palm" and ironic "calm." In the penultimate stanza the poet repeats "caress," reinforces it with "flesh," "bless," "pressure," then creates the shocking contrast, in sound and sense, of "hot / cowards," and ends with the "all-wall" rhyme from the poem's opening, now fearsomely resonant, and the "do–blue–through" rhymes, and at last the "night," "tight," and final "right." These sound-links lace the poem into a tight unity even while its subject is the loss of unity. They also add a slight tone of levity to the dominant tone of intense attention and devotion—an intensifying device like the jokes in Ginsberg's "Howl."

"Bleeding" and "Feel Me" have in common, technically, a white line cutting the text. This happens often in *Iconographs*, and I will not belabor the possibility that "inner space" may be available as actual substance to a woman poet in a way that it might not be to her brother. The point is that in both poems, space *is* substantial. It stands in the verbal rhythm for hesita-

Feel Me

"Feel me to do right," our father said
on his   death bed. We did not quite
 know-- in fact, not at all-- what he meant.
His last whisper was spent as through a slot in a wall.
He left us a key, but how did it
fit? "Feel me
         to do right." Did it mean

that, though he died, he would be felt
     through some aperture, or by some unseen instrument
our dad just then had come
     to know? So, to do right always, we need but feel his
        spirit? Or was it merely
     his apology for dying? "Feel that I
      do right in not trying, as you insist, to stay

              on your side. There is the wide
        gateway and the splendid tower,
and you implore me to wait here, with the worms!"
        Had he defined his terms, and could we discriminate
        among his motives, we might
     have found out how to "do right" before we died-- supposing
              he felt he suddenly knew

              what dying was.
              "You do wrong because you do not feel
as I do now" was maybe the sense. "Feel me, and emulate
           my state, for I am becoming less dense--
           I am feeling right, for the first
time." And then the vessel burst, and we were kneeling
                   around an emptiness.

                   We cannot feel our
         father now. His power courses through us, yes, but he--
           the chest and cheek, the foot and palm,
           the mouth of oracle-- is calm. And we still seek
                   his meaning. "Feel me," he said,
           and emphasized that word.
           Should we have heard it as a plea

              for a caress-- A constant caress,
        since flesh to flesh was all that we could do right
        if we would bless him? The dying must feel
                   the pressure of that
              question-- lying flat, turning cold
              from brow to heel-- the hot
                   cowards there above

              protesting their love, and saying
                   "What can we do? Are you all
                        right?" While the wall opens
                   and the blue night pours through. "What
              can we do? We want to do what's right."
     "Lie down with me, and hold me, tight. Touch me. Be
              with me. Feel with me. Feel me, to do right."

tion, a gap the voice must leap in every line. It slows the tempo, enforces stillness, makes room for meditation. Visually it "means" separation, as if, between the knife and the cut, between the living and the dying, between experience and the ability to comprehend experience, falls this white shadow. Emotionally, the space expresses that sadness, appropriately wordless, which we feel in the face of all disunity we wish to heal but—so far, so ill—recognize we cannot.

In Swenson's more typical vein of natural observation and wonderment, but still intimately concerned with relationships and connections, here is a lovely piece about sky and sea, or about time and space.

A trail of stars, a shoreline, the silhouette of a flying bird, the idea of reflection. Yet notice that the reflection, the symmetry, is not exact, as the poem thins out toward its close, just as a reflection in moving water can only sketchily duplicate its object, and just as our position in the galaxy makes it impossible for us to imagine "other watchers" as substantial as ourselves. The absoluteness of presence versus distance, which is in Einsteinian rather than Newtonian physics, has entered this poem's form. "Fire Island" also illustrates the fact that the shapes in *Iconographs* are commonly agreeable to look at, but never because of a mechanical symmetry. Order shapes these poems, but so do pinches of disorder and randomness. If one margin of a poem forms a straight line or a simple curve, another is ragged. If sentences are simple, line-breaks cut their syntax unexpectedly. Where rhyme occurs it does so irregularly, or if the rhyme and meter are regular, then the pattern imposed breaks up and disguises them. In other words, Swenson has taken care to make her poems by the same principles— mixing Law and Chance—which we believe nature itself employs to make all of its objects, from DNA molecules to clusters of galaxies.

The second half of *Iconographs,* located as the poet has become located on Long Island, contains eleven poems taking place around water, some describing scenes, some exploring the action of water on objects—a boat stave, a bottle, a stick. One states a rule for water, and more.

```
                         F
                         I
                         R
                         E
                       I S L A N D

                       The Milky Way
                     above, the milky
                     waves beside,
                      when the sand is night
                      the sea is galaxy.
                    The unseparate stars
                  mark a twining coast
               with phosphorescent
            surf
          in the black sky's trough.
      Perhaps we walk on black
   star ash, and watch
the milks of light foam forward, swish and spill
      while other watchers, out
        walking in their white
           great
             swerve,
               gather
                   our
                      low
                        spark,
                        our little Way
                          the dark
                          glitter
                           in
                             their
                             s
                              i
                               g
                                h
                                 t
                                  .
```

"To generalize is to be an idiot," says William Blake. To generalize about "everything" takes some temerity. Still, the sight of this extraordinary poem may persuade us first that it offers an authentic picture of the activity of waves, and then that this interdependence of impulses, "to happen" and "not to happen," with the quiescence and stasis between, defines organic as well as inorganic motion—defines the growth of plants, animals, humans, the flux of human creativity (Swenson has said this poem happened after a period of writer's block), the surges and withdrawals of anyone's emotional and intellectual life. Even the motions of history: revolution, counter-revolution, revolution.

Visually exciting where it depicts the strong positive and negative forces, visually dull (though the dynamic of the whole depends on that dull still point) where it depicts stasis, the poem seems to flash our desires on its screen like an X ray. My apologies to Swenson in case she did not mean all this, but my gratitude anyway. Situated in a little historical trough, as we Americans at present are, perhaps melancholy about our incapacity to "stack up" to anything, we may find this a heartening and promising poem. For once, a credible upbeat ending!

Some final points about the method of *Iconographs*. If all poetry approaches metaphor insofar as it creates verbal equivalents for nonverbal experience, then consciously shaped poetry is a sort of P^2—poetry raised by one power. First the experience or perception, then the text necessary to state the experience and all its implications truly, then a visual shape related to both. Swenson distinguishes her method of composition from that of concrete poetry by insisting that the text of each poem comes first, and can be considered complete and self-sufficient before the shapes are found. Shape then becomes a metaphor, enriching language as language enriches experience. But where concrete poems typically, and deliberately, have no interest separable from the visual, the technique in *Iconographs* maintains distinctions. Perhaps we should call it an art of simile rather than metaphor. Word and picture do not fuse, any more than the special sensations offered by our ear and eye can ever become one sensation, or any more than

How Everything Happens
(Based on a Study of the Wave)

```
                                                happen.
                                             to
                                          up
                                 stacking
                               is
                      something
When nothing is happening


When it happens
             something
                       pulls
                             back
                                 not
                                    to
                                       happen.



When                             has happened.
      pulling back       stacking up
               happens


      has happened                             stacks up.
When it               something             nothing
                         pulls back while



Then nothing is happening.


                                 happens.
                              and
                        forward
                   pushes
                 up
            stacks
      something
Then
```

the external world we behold and the internal world which beholds it can ever become one. Connection exists instead of identity, tantalizing and delighting.

Form in the history of poetry always comes back, more or less consciously, to an imitation of form in the natural world, prior to all art, which all art celebrates. The fluidity of Elizabethan song relates directly to a literal belief in the harmonious music of the spheres. Eighteenth-century English poetry was rigid because the eighteenth-century idea of natural law was exclusively mechanical. When the Romantics decided that Nature equaled spontaneity, Coleridge said poetic form had to be organic, like a tree, not like a machine. Keats wanted verse with the "full-throated ease" of a nightingale. Shelley wanted it "unpremeditated" like the skylark's song, or like the West Wind, or like the spontaneous utterances of a wind harp. To justify the liberty of his poetry, Whitman said its verses were modeled on the ocean waves.

The formal fragmentation of most "free verse" reflects not only the social and political incoherence poets have found in our century, but a loss of the belief that nature offers us models of significant form. "Yet for all this," as Hopkins once wrote, "Nature is never spent." We may be coming around to a rediscovery, and a finer understanding, of natural laws and natural freedoms, and our position within them. Olsen asked that the poem "take its place alongside the things of nature." Without theorizing about this, Swenson shows one way, formally-informally, to express our relation to the natural world:

> We, who through her textures move,
> we specks upon her glass,
> who try to place, relate and name
> all things within her mass.

NOTES

1. All poems in this essay are quoted from *New & Selected Things Taking Place* (New York: Little, Brown and Co., 1978), with the

exception of poems quoted from *Iconographs* (New York: Scribner, 1970).

2. Elizabeth Bishop, letter to May Swenson, Nov. 13, 1962.
3. Anthony Hecht in the *New York Review of Books* 1, no. 2 (Spring 1963): 33; X. J. Kennedy in *Poetry* (February 1964):330.

Her Cargo

Adrienne Rich and the Common Language

I.

Adrienne Rich is a poet of ideas.

In most poetic circles, it is unfashionable to espouse ideas—except, of course, fór ideas about technique. There exists in America a national poetry industry owned and operated by skilled poetic technicians, hundreds, perhaps thousands of whom write flawlessly, and they all agree that form is an extension of content. Yet to discuss the nature and implications of the philosophical and moral positions in most American poems would be like discussing the tastiness of *papier-mâché* apples and oranges. The pieces resemble fruit marvelously to the eye. Other cardboard fruit makers examine and enjoy and rank them. Young disciple fruit makers come to schools to learn the craft. There is considerable complaining that the public does not want to buy, which is understood to be the defect of the public. On a vastly expanded scale, we have an equivalent to Pope's "mob of gentlemen who wrote with ease." For minor critics as well as minor poets, the identification of poetry with craftsmanship is comforting.

A difference between major and minor poetry is that the former announces ideas, the latter fills in the blanks.

> *I celebrate myself and sing myself,*
> *And what I assume you shall assume,*
> *For every atom belonging to me as good belongs to you.*

That is an idea.

Hypocrite lecteur, mon semblable, mon frère!

That is another.

> *Your mother dead and you unborn,*
> *your two hands grasping your head,*
> *drawing it down against the blade of life,*
> *your nerves the nerves of a midwife*
> *learning her trade.*

That is another, of a comparable magnitude. It manifests a serious and therefore arguable set of assertions about the actual world outside its art, and demands, as ideas in poetry so often demand: you must change your life. The lines come from Rich's "The Mirror in Which Two Are Seen as One." Like Whitman's and Baudelaire's, these lines depend on the assumption that the writer's mind exists to embody the implicit meaning of a culture at a moment in time, the place history has marched to, intelligence at its keenest pitch; and to bring the reader there. They declare a state of awakened consciousness—the poet's—and claim that the present actual consciousness of the writer, and the latent consciousness of the reader, are identical.

Whitman asks us to think that we are innocent and great. Baudelaire asks us to think that we are guilty and wearily disgusted. Rich asks us to think that we need to give birth to ourselves.

Thought in poetry lives by its metaphors. There is an echo here of Matthew Arnold's Victorian lament that he lived between "two worlds, one dead, the other powerless to be born," an idea with which Rich agrees so forcefully and angrily that she transforms the figure to its opposite.[1] By "worlds," Arnold meant civilizations. Rich refuses to see present and potential civilizations as "worlds" in some cosmic void remote from each other and from us, distinct from the individual will. As a woman, she reexamines the birth metaphor in a way that would astonish Arnold. A healthy civilization might give birth to another as a live mother gives birth to a live child. A healthy individual mother might have living powers engaged in the maturation of her young. But as things are, Rich says, we must be born again by our own agency. We can and must give birth to ourselves, create ourselves. Moreover, to give birth is naturally a feminine activity. (An implication is that if *men* want to struggle into life and not die stillborn in the womb of that old bitch gone in the teeth, that botched civilization, they will have to feminize themselves.) It requires not Christlike wounded surgeons plying the steel, not Confucian philosopher-kings, but midwives. The midwife is an important figure in Rich because she lacks social status, lacks patriarchal apparatus, and comes from a buried, barely surviving tradition of powerful working females. By rediscovering this tradition, women will grow strong.

Does the reader agree with the poet? The reader cannot think: oh, it is only *poetry*. One grapples with Rich, one wrestles and hugs, one agrees and disagrees intensely.

II.

The poet springs from the soil of Modernism. Her youthful writing in *A Change of World* (1951) and *The Diamond Cutters* (1955) reflects the ranking styles in postwar literary academe. From Frost and Auden in particular she inherits craftsmanly formalism, an analytical rather than emotional treatment of material, and a resigned sense of life as a diminished thing. "We had to take the world as it was given," she says regretfully in neat pentameter, while an emotion more violent than resignation stirs beneath the surface.

Failures of language, standing for failures of love, appear at key points in these first two volumes. Superficially, the young poet's handling of this theme seems conventional enough. The modern era, or one strand of it, begins with Eliot-Prufrock irritably exclaiming, "It is impossible to say just what I mean!" That words have no privileged hold on reality, that we are alienated beings who cannot say what we "mean" because our existence lacks meaning, that we strain and fail to communicate with each other—these have become commonplace propositions, almost, indeed, cliché. They refer, if we like, to the Decline of the West, a concept filtering down from Spengler to the democratic masses, which all America learns about in "The Sounds of Silence," soundtracking a film called *The Graduate* in which one world is dead, another powerless to be born. (If the film proposes dewy-eyed romance as the plausible solution to the wasteland it depicts, that is because the left hand of a work of art may not know what the right hand is doing, and Happy Ever After dies hard.) Rich has "the unsaid word" of a wife in loyal stasis while her husband ranges. There are uncommunicating parental figures in "The Middle-Aged." A woman who "thought that life was different than it is" goes down to old age mildly, unprotesting. "Living in Sin," a poem of Lowellian distaste for shabby reality, depicts the tainting of romance by common grime; but the heroine says nothing.

Some of these poems tremble on the brink of indignation. They seem about to state explicitly the pattern they all share, of a connection between feminine subordination in male-dominated middle-class relationships, and emotionally lethal inarticulateness for both sexes. But the poetry in these two books is minor because it is polite. It illustrates symptoms but does not probe causes. There is no disputing the ideas of the predecessors, and Adrienne Rich at this point is a cautious good poet in the sense of being a good girl, a quality noted with approval by her early reviewers.

In the essay "When We Dead Awaken," Rich recalls years of silence and dissatisfaction with this early poetry, years of marriage, three sons, outward normality and private depression, despair, guilt, which she retrospectively interprets as a conflict between the subversive demands of the poetic imagination and the demands placed by society and by herself on a woman trying to live "in the old way":

> I had thought I was choosing a full life: the life available to most men, in which sexuality, work, and parenthood could coexist.

But I felt, at 29, guilt toward the people closest to me, and guilty toward my own being. . . . The fifties and early sixties were years of rapid revelations: the sit-ins and marches in the South, the Bay of Pigs, the early anti-war movement, raised large questions—questions for which the masculine world of the academy around me seemed to have expert and fluent answers. But I needed desperately to think for myself. . . . I was looking desperately for clues, because if there were no clues then I thought I might be insane.[2]

One clue was evidently Simone de Beauvoir's *The Second Sex*, first published in the United States in 1953, which defines woman in patriarchal society as the perennial Object, doomed to immanence and passivity, blocked from activity and transcendence, trained and imprisoned in the exclusive vocation of love, expected to be happy, forbidden to be free. De Beauvoir's feminism and existentialism stand behind *Snapshots of a Daughter-in-Law* (1963), Rich's breakthrough volume.

The title poem of *Snapshots* was the first Rich wrote openly as "a female poet" although she had not found "the courage . . . to use the pronoun 'I'—the woman in the poem is always 'she.'"[3] The young woman speaker sees all women as "pinned down by love," and thinks she is going mad. But her real subject is the woman of intellect. Mary Wollstonecraft appears as

> a woman partly brave and partly good,
> who fought with what she partly understood.
> Few men around her could or would do more.
> Hence she was labelled harpy, shrew, and whore.

Sister writers have been encouraged in graceful timidity and mediocrity:

> Our blight has been our sinecure . . .
> slattern thought styled intuition,
> every lapse forgiven, our crime
> only to cast too bold a shadow
> or smash the mold straight off.

For that, solitary confinement,
tear gas, attrition shelling.
Few applicants for that honor.

"A thinking woman sleeps with monsters," Rich discovers.
"The beak that grips her, she becomes." The culture of the
past is a predator to a woman; an intellectual woman who
absorbs it becomes her own enemy. Thus for the first time in
this poem, Rich challenges the language of the past, quoting
Cicero, Horace, Campion, Diderot, Johnson, Shakespeare—as
the flattering, insulting, condescending enemies of women's
intellect. "Dulce ridens, dulce loquens"—Horace's lady sweetly
laughing, sweetly speaking, is a lady who shaves her legs to
gleam "like petrified mammoth-tusk" for male pleasure. Final-
ly the poet imagines a new woman:

> She's long about her coming, who must be
> more merciless to herself than history.
> Her mind full to the wind, I see her plunge
> breasted and glancing through the currents,
> taking the light upon her
> at least as beautiful as any boy
> or helicopter
>   poised, still coming
> her fine blades making the air wince
> but her cargo
> no promise then:
> delivered
> palpable
> ours.

"Snapshots" consists of fragmentary and odd-shaped sections
instead of stanzas, and has the immediacy and force Rich did
not attempt earlier. In the same volume, "The Knight" ana-
lyzes that traditional masculinity which superficially glorifies
but internally destroys man, just as the role of sweet laugher,
sweet speaker destroys woman. A prisoner of his chain mail,
"only his eye is living,/a lump of bitter jelly/set in a metal
mask." In "Ghost of a Chance" a man "trying to think" is like a

fish attempting an evolutionary leap from sea to air. "Prospective Immigrants Please Note" reminds the reader at the threshold of liberty how we dread what we desire: "There is always the risk / of remembering your name" and "The door makes no promises. / It is only a door." The violence against women's minds and men's emotions in our culture, the need to free ourselves, the risk, the internal impediments, the pain—these will be primary themes.

After *Snapshots*, nothing inhibits Rich's intensity or integrity. The feeling of something inexplicably wrong has been transformed into cries that the house is on fire, and the mind of the poet is ablaze. Writing as a woman who can trust only the inner voice, because every external voice will echo the demand of "dulce ridens, dulce loquens," she explores the experience of an "I" which is increasingly the "we" of female consciousness present and past. *Necessities of Life* (1966) concerns the necessity of personal withdrawal and reconstruction: "I used myself, let nothing use me," as a prerequisite for life in the world. Outside, things fall apart: "They're tearing down, tearing up / this city, block by block. / Rooms cut in half / hang like flayed carcasses." The physical body, she recognizes, should give pleasure:

> lust too is a jewel
> a sweet flower and what
> pure happiness to know
> all our high-toned questions
> breed in a lively animal.

Yet neither lust nor love works in practice: "Miscarried knowledge twists us / like hot sheets thrown askew." Parents, husband, friends, siblings, children—all relationships are a wrestling "old as sickheartedness, / modern as pure annihilation." *Leaflets* (1969) and *The Will to Change* (1971) extend the field of struggle and intensify the sense of crisis. Confronting not only Vietnam but the barricades of class, race, sex, youth versus age, activist versus theorist, Rich cannot accept either a public or a private life not motivated by the will to change oneself, to change others, to change the world. She wants

> life without caution
> the only worth living . . .
> that self-defense be not
> the arm's first motion

The tempo of the work speeds to reflect the speeding mind. Divesting herself of traditional formalities, the poet lets herself think in (apparently) disconnected streaks. "The notes for the poem are the only poem," she says. "The moment of change is the only poem." There are gestures in the direction of hope: "I am thinking how we can use what we have / to invent what we need." A few pieces—"Women," "The Observer," "Planetarium"—suggest strength through some connection between woman and the world of nature. But mostly the will is paralyzed by the monstrosity of evil it faces. Nothing seems alterable except by violence. In poem after poem, every outer atrocity is an inner one:

> O God I am not spiritless
>   but a spirit can be stunned,
>   a battery felt going dead . . .
> > ["The Key," *Leaflets*]

> I'd rather
> taste blood, yours or mine, flowing
> from a sudden slash, than cut all day
> with blunt scissors on the dotted line
> like the teacher told.
> > ["On Edges," *Leaflets*]

> my body is a list of wounds
> symmetrically placed
> a village
> blown open by bombs
> that did not finish the job

By *Diving Into the Wreck* (1973), Rich's ideas have become systematically feminist, and she is assuming an influential position in an intellectual movement which is coming to include not only Anglo-American writers such as Millett, Greer, Daly,

Piercy, and Olsen, but the contemporary French feminists Hélène Cixous, Monique Wittig, Luce Iragaray, and Marguerite Duras. The constellation of institutions which comprise patriarchy is held responsible for all imperialisms, political and psychic. Our civilization's religion, philosophy, history, law and literature rest on the subordination of women and of the female principle in men, and our civilization is therefore finished:

> The tragedy of sex
> lies around us, a woodlot
> the axes are sharpened for.
> The old shelters and huts . . .
> scenes of masturbation
> and dirty jokes.
> A man's world. But finished.
> They themselves have sold it to the machines.
> ["Waking in the Dark," *Diving Into the Wreck*]

Perceiving an omnipresent male dread of impotence which informs her interpretation of high culture, Rich hears Beethoven's Ninth Symphony

> trying to tell something the man
> does not want out, would keep if he could
> gagged and bound and flogged with chords of Joy
> where everything is silence and the
> beating of a bloody fist upon
> a splintered table
> ["The Ninth Symphony of Beethoven Understood at
> Last as a Sexual Message," *Diving Into the Wreck*]

The "compromised" woman who continues to live in this society finds herself envying

> the freedom of the wholly mad
> to smear & play with her madness
> write with her fingers dipped in it . . .
> ["The Phenomenology of Anger," *Diving Into the Wreck*]

She nevertheless continues to take the risk and suffer the pain of self-knowledge:

> If I am flesh sunning on rock
> if I am brain burning in fluorescent light
>
> if I am dream like a wire with fire
> throbbing along it
>
> if I am death to man
> I have to know it
>
> ["August," *Diving Into the Wreck*]

She identifies with other women and attempts to understand their common history in order to organize a collective, not an individual, escape, in which the traditional dualisms of Western philosophy and literature will be transcended. Philosophically, the feminism in Rich points toward acts of synthesis. Body and spirit must be conceived and experienced in unity. Personal and political life are metaphors for each other: "The moment when a feeling enters a body / Is political. This touch is political." The values of subjectivity, emotionality and empathy are to be conjoined with, not divided from, those of rationality. Finally, of course, life and art must coincide, without self-insulation or self-protection; all else is hypocrisy.

The poet thinks in images, and Rich's gift for vivid and energetic imagery has been one of her chief strengths since the beginning. Her range includes astronomy, modern technology, natural history, movies (e.g., the movie imagery in *The Will to Change,* where new-wave film becomes a major metaphor for the documenting of life), historical records, as well as the contemporary urban scene and domestic setting. She uses dream and fantasy images extensively. Her primary subject is herself battling "the beak that grips her," which is the male culture's denial of her identity, and her language functions at a level where her life and the lives of others evidently coincide. If we look at the poetry American women have been writing for the last two decades and want to delineate their discoveries, it is Rich, over and over again, who says a thing most plainly, most memorably—because she has understood it.

Throughout the period subsequent to *Snapshots*, Rich questions the idea of language and the value of poetry, exemplifying the conflicts "a thinking woman," whose tools are words, undergoes when she wants expression of personal truth and communication of realities hitherto unrecognized. She needs to be what the French critic Claudine Herrman has recently called *voleuse de langue*—a thief of language, a female Prometheus—because literature from her point of view is corrupt, its conventions having evolved out of experiences which exclude hers; at its best it consistently upholds values alien to her own.

What Rich does with this problem comes in three stages, corresponding to her phases of self-reconstruction, political engagement, and feminism. In the first two, I think she hits dead ends. In the last, she begins to discover an alternative. *Necessities of Life* takes as model Emily Dickinson's retreat from "the air buzzing with spoiled language" to the house in Amherst:

> and in your half-cracked way you chose
> silence for entertainment
> chose to have it out at last
> on your own premises.
>
> ["I Am in Danger—Sir"]

"Half-cracked" was what Dickinson's hoped-for mentor, Higginson, stupidly considered her to be: another eccentric poetess. But what else could a woman with "a man's mind" be, in nineteenth century New England? What should she be, unable to make private and public selves cohere, but cracked, divided? "Have it out" signifies expression but also combat. "Premises" beautifully means both the house in Amherst and the poet's personal assumptions about her life. There is wit here, as well as courage and toughness. Still, retreat is retreat. Dickinson could have her premises, but she could not say "What I assume you shall assume." Being a woman of genius meant paying a price: isolation. In *Leaflets* and *The Will to Change*, the poet reenters the world with the desire to use language for healing, but is repeatedly defeated. "Images for Godard" sees "language as city" surrounded by shockproof suburbs and squatters awaiting eviction—a place out of touch with reality. "A Valediction Forbidding Mourning" has "my swirling wants. Your frozen lips./The grammar turned and attacked me." "The Burning of Paper Instead of Children" juxtaposes the idea of book-burning by two schoolboys, which has shocked a liberal neighbor, against the literal burning of Jeanne d'Arc and the napalming of Vietnam. And there are other kinds of burning, such as slavery, poverty, injustice, sexual loneliness: "there are books that describe all this/and they are useless." Worse than useless; blameworthy. Attacking not only the formal language of the past but that of the present—however well intentioned—Rich prefers a child's semiliterate composition on poverty, or Artaud's *burn the texts.* "This is the oppressor's language/yet I need it to talk to you. . . . I cannot touch you and this is the oppressor's language," she concludes in desperation. Two years later, in the title poem of *Diving into the Wreck,* a new possibility opens. There is a breakthrough comparable to that of "Snapshots."

The poet in "Diving" reads but cannot use "the book of myths" in which "our names do not appear." She seeks "the thing itself and not the myth," which sounds like an extension of the anti-intellectualism of the *Leaflets* and *Will to Change* period. But this is a different sort of poem from anything earlier. For one thing, it is narrative. The poet does not remain trapped in stasis and analysis, helplessly acted upon. She makes a move; she acts. For another, her language is revisionist. Out of the past, she invents an altered symbolism.

From Homer onward, quests in Western male literature orient themselves either heroically outward toward conquest or spiritually upward toward transcendence. A hero is a *superior* being, and the metaphors which define his deeds are upwardly mobile. When heroes (Odysseus, Hercules, Aeneas, Christ, Dante, the narrator of *Paradise Lost*) descend, it is to hell, and they re-ascend. Mountaintops are favored locales for visionary experience. Rich herself in "Snapshots" envisioned an aerial new woman. But here, she goes down; the poem repeats this point. She enters water. At first she blacks out, but then:

> the sea is not a question of power
> I have to learn alone
> to turn my body without force
> in the deep element.

Not a question of power; *without* force: a female quest, a female form of heroism. The sea may mean the poet's personal past, or her subconscious, or those of her race: it is her "element," her identity, which she need not combat. What Rich finds amid "the damage . . . and the treasures" is her deepest self. This is no longer "I" but an androgynous naked mermaid-armored merman: "I am she . . . I am he . . ." and finally a plural identification with the wreck itself:

> we are the half-destroyed instruments
> that once held to a course
> the water-eaten log
> the fouled compass
>
> We are, I am, you are
> by cowardice or courage
> the one who find our way
> back to this scene

If the source of an oppressor's language is a set of false perceptions of reality, it is necessary to begin at the beginning. The poem suggests a place, a scene, where our iron distinctions between perceiver and perceived, subject and object, he and she, I and you, dissolve. There it leaves us.

III.

"The Phenomenology of Anger," that extraordinary poem which opens by invoking "the freedom of the wholly mad," contains the following passage:

> I would have loved to live in a world
> of women and men gaily
> in collusion with green leaves, stalks,
> building mineral cities, transparent domes,
> little huts of woven grass
> each with its own pattern—
> a conspiracy to coexist
> with the Crab Nebula, the exploding
> universe, the Mind—

The thought breaks off here. The poet has already defined an "enemy," a "prince of air and darkness" who is at once insensitive lover, defoliator of fields, killer in Vietnam. It goes on in the next section to quote a woman saying she has never felt "real love" for anyone but children and other women; in this context, Rich asks us to reconsider "Botticelli's Venus, Kali, / the Judith of Chartres / with her so-called smile."

We may compare the passage above with a poem by one of Rich's early models. This is from the conclusion to W. H. Auden's sonnet sequence "In War Time":

> Wandering lost upon the mountains of our choice,
> Again and again we sigh for an ancient South,
> For the warm nude ages of instinctive poise,
> For the taste of joy in the innocent mouth . . .
>
> We envy streams and houses that are sure:
> But we are articled to error; we
> Were never nude and calm like a great door,
> And never will be perfect like the fountains;
> We live in freedom by necessity,
> A mountain people dwelling among mountains.

The difference between the passages are striking. Auden's musicality celebrates an ordered and beautiful natural world. Rich's rhymeless and uneven verse, the hardness of her imagery, the uncompleted sentence, signify alienation from whatever design may structure the universe. Again, Auden's "South" presupposes a literate ear's memory of a pastoral tradition reaching back through, say, Keats' "Nightingale Ode"

("O for a beaker full of the warm South . . . dance, and Provençal song, and country mirth") to Arcadia and the garden of Genesis. Auden allows some sort of authenticity to this tradition, even if only imaginative and never historical. Rich, on the other hand, does not believe that such a life as she desires existed in the past, nor does she accept the dreamy reverberations of a literary tradition (belonging to the language of the oppressor) which would pretend it did. Auden's humanistic "we" is Rich's isolated "I," who does not imagine anyone else sharing her ideals. Finally and most significantly, where Auden accepts human destiny as fallen and failing, endowing our fate with pathos and yet with a sense of heroism and nobility, Rich has only the dry stems of a verb tense denoting impossibility. Not "I would love to live" but "I would *have* loved." To imagine a balance between nature and humanity, city and country, technology and the primitive, woman and man, proves too great a strain. She cannot say "harmony" but must say "collusion," must say "conspiracy to coexist," as if nature and humanity were negotiating nations something like Russia and the United States.

If Auden's and Rich's versions of pastoral constitute a choice between accepting and rejecting a consoling illusion, one should concur in the rejection. Better the sour truth than a sweet lie. Nevertheless, two aspects of "The Phenomenology of Anger," and the bulk of Rich's work in her mature period, provoke questions both poetic and moral.

Why, in Rich's writing, does one find so little joy, so little sense of the power of joy? Why does the work come from a sense of unrelieved crisis in which nothing can be celebrated, nothing savored? Rich is not, one feels, a poet to whom love— untheoretical, undoctrinal love—comes easily, either toward herself or toward others. She does not employ memories of childhood wholeness. She does not construct desirable fantasies. There is suffering, and then there is more suffering, with "no imagination to forestall woe," almost as if suffering itself were a value. In this respect Rich differs from feminists like Marge Piercy and Robin Morgan, Alta and Judy Grahn, whose work suggests that women's sense of their own wholeness, and the gladness that accompanies wholeness, is indispensable for a feminist revolution. To journey with Rich is to travel painfully in the wilderness, to be warned against the fleshpots of Egypt and the golden calf, to feel the backward drag of slavery, and to struggle with all one's might against it. But the struggle requires a vision. Rich's readers need to know about the female equivalent of the burning bush, the voice of the covenant, the promised land. They need to know about the goddess. Lacking the imagination's projection of a world without victims, a self unvictimized, unmastered, complete—and it is for the poets to give us this, to articulate the delight that is *there*, latently, as much as women's despair is *there*—lacking this, the will to change is helplessly fettered.

A more dismaying aspect of Rich's work to me is her partisanship. Explicitly or implicitly, since *Snapshots*, Rich's position has depended on the idea of an enemy. Her "I" affirms by excluding, her communal "we" implies a hostile "they." Of course "we" know who "they" are. For a period after *Snapshots* the poet uses male figures sympathetically; there are poems of kindness and hopefulness addressed to her husband; there is Orion, her brother-double; there are friend/lover figures in *Leaflets*, and the male artists Chekhov, Ghalib, Rodin, Berrigan, Artaud, Godard in *Leaflets* and *The Will to Change*. In *Diving* the poet defines herself as the androgyne, the being who is at once female and male. But men in this volume are depicted universally and exclusively as parasitic on women, emotionally threatened by them, brutal—the cop is identified with the rapist—and undeserving of pity. "His" mind is a nightmare of possessiveness, conquest and mysogyny. The poet in "The Phenomenology of Anger" dreams of killing this man, but killing is

> not enough. When I dream of meeting
> the enemy, this is my dream:
>
> white acetylene
> ripples from my body

effortlessly released
perfectly trained
on the true enemy

raking his body down to the thread
of existence
burning away his lie
leaving him in a new
world; a changed
man

I hope not to oversimplify this issue. Women's anger is real, and it is legitimate. We see it surfacing everywhere in women's writing, the best and the worst (I suppose it is missing only from the mediocre), like a scream from a mouth that has just been ungagged. This anger needs acknowledgment. Unacknowledged, it poisons and cripples. But when an angry woman implies that she fantasizes punishing her enemy purely for his own good, she begins to resemble the officer who said he burned the village to save it. It is pleasant and self-deceptive to feel that "I" or "we" are violent only in response to "their" violence. It is pleasant to believe that aggressiveness, competitiveness, selfishness, egotism, violence, are "their" characteristics, not mine. The unfortunate truth is that they are human characteristics. The liberated will find these impulses newly released within themselves, and may want to take responsibility for them.

If patriarchy denies a woman's full humanity, does that force her to retaliate in kind? Suppose that we read a famous seventeenth-century text:

No man is an island, entire of itself; every man is a piece of the continent, a part of the main. If a clod be washed away from the sea, Europe is the less, as well as if a promontory were, as well as if a manor of thy friend's or thy own were. Any man's death diminishes me because I am involved in mankind, and therefore never send to know for whom the bell tolls; it tolls for thee.

We must stop using "man," "mankind," for the generic "human." We must understand that John Donne did not value women as portions of the human species in quite the way he did men; nor did anyone in the seventeenth century. We must notice Donne's not-coincidental allegiance to the class of landed gentry. Rich teaches these lessons. Another kind of gauntlet is flung down in "From an Old House in America," a poem recollecting the history of American women as breeding-mares, witches, isolated from one another on the frontier: "her hand unconscious on the cradle . . . his mother-hatred driving him / into exile from the earth. . . ." The poet, attempting to find their meaning for herself, interrupts herself with an imagined dialogue:

> *But can't you see me as a human being*
> he said
>
> *What is a human being*
> she said
>
> *I try to understand*
> he said
>
> *What will you undertake*
> she said
>
> *Will you punish me for history*
> he said
>
> *What will you undertake*
> she said . . .

Rich's "he" unquestionably exists: a good, defensive liberal, unwilling to undertake the spiritual transformation feminism demands of him. Is he indeed Everyman? And what of the poet? "Any woman's death diminishes me," is her concluding line, duplicating and perpetuating the dualism which feminist theory might seek to destroy. *Separatism*—that is the creation of a category of nonpersons—is hardly an original thing in this century.

These elements in Rich's work dismay me, I must add, for several reasons. First, Rich is the strongest woman poet in the country, and a major influence. If she is in error, her influence serves error. Second, whatever distresses me in Rich—the joylessness, the self-pity, the self-righteousness, exists also within myself and within others. She is a mirror in which multitudes are seen as one. Third, she may not be in error. If this is the case, we are emerging from the tangled growths of the past, only to enter a desert which appears to stretch indefinitely before us, arid and stony, and none of us will see the end of it in our lifetimes.

IV.

The Dream of a Common Language at last gives us Rich as visionary. "Dream" implies this. "Language" means not only words, poetry—several of the poems are about "a whole new poetry"—but any form of communication, including the touch of bodies, and including silence. It means the ability "to name the world" essential for gaining strength in the world; and "the drive / to connect," through symbols and in actuality, with each other, the world, and ourselves. "Common" language means a faith that attempts to communicate can succeed, that we can connect, not as privileged persons or under special circumstances, but in ordinary dailiness.

The core of the book is its exploration of loving woman-to-woman relationships. Rich speaks of mothers and daughters, literal and figurative sisters, cohorts in poetry, lovers, ancestresses. She sees all women as actually or potentially conjoined by a common love-memory of a mother's body:

> our faces dreaming hour on hour
> in the salt smell of her lap . . .
> how she floated great and tender in our dark . . .
> and how we thought she loved
> the strange male body first
> that took, that took, whose taking seemed a law . . .
>   And how beneath
> the strange male bodies
> we sank in terror or in resignation . . .

"Sibling Mysteries," from which this passage comes, traces Rich's eroticism:

> the daughters never were
> true brides of the father
>
> the daughters were to begin with
> brides of the mother
>
> then brides of each other
> under a different law
>
> let me hold you and tell you

As a flute song of personal meditation, "Sibling Mysteries" is hauntingly lovely. As a myth of female sexuality, it is too narrow. Yes, women's initial erotic experiences are maternal-infantile. So are men's. Yes, perhaps mature sexuality attempts to recover and replay the blissful mother-child union. Perhaps all adult tenderness, all affection, finds its source and models itself on those memories. This idea could explain a great deal about human romance—not confined to love between women.[4] For some women, the stereotypic dominant-father/subordinate-mother family pattern does not apply. For some, the physicality of our mothers never stopped being available. And for some, heterosexual experience has never meant terror or resignation; on the contrary. William Blake's *Notebook* contains a short poem entitled "The Question Answered":

> What is it men in women do require?
> The lineaments of Gratified Desire.
> What is it women do in men require?
> The lineaments of Gratified Desire.

Age twenty, I became a Blakean when I read this. I find the Lesbian Imperative offensively totalitarian, and would prefer to defend human diversity as well as human liberty.

Three other poems in *Dream* excite my skepticism. The opening pieces on Marie Curie and Elvira Shatayev appear to romanticize feminine martyrdom; the latter is an all-female *liebestod.* Where is the portrait of a woman whose power kills neither others nor herself? "Hunger" seems marred by a naive belief that women's love, "hosed" on the world, would eliminate its literal and figurative famines. Those who believe in infallible feminine virtue may recall the comparable virtue of the American Worker in the 1930s.

These are comparatively tangential matters, not vitiating this volume's courageous spirit, its transformations, the beauty of its poetry. The force of love, negligible in her earlier books, here brings Rich a resolution to trust, to move from victimization toward responsibility and choice, and to reject (notwithstanding the aura of the first two poems) martyrdom:

> I believe I am choosing something new
> not to suffer uselessly

she says in one poem; and in another,

> the woman who cherished
> her suffering is dead. I am her descendant.
> I love the scar-tissue she handed on to me
> but I want to go on from here with you
> fighting the temptation to make a career of pain.

Rich's fear lest she "use" those she loves in the old way of sexual (or literary) exploitation is scarcely a traditional theme in love poetry; it might well become so. Both in the book's central section of twenty-one love poems, and in the framing poems around them, one senses not simply the will to change but the accomplishment.

The most important poems break new ground metaphorically. "Origins and History of Consciousness," opening in the poet's crisis-haunted room, moves to a dream of walking into water:

> My bare feet are numbed already by the snow
> but the water
> is mild, I sink and float

like a warm, amphibious animal
that has broken the net, has run
through fields of snow leaving no print;
this water washes off the scent—
you are clear now
of the hunter, the trapper
the wardens of the mind—

This of course recalls "Diving Into the Wreck," but the speaker of "Diving" needed props—rubber suit, knife, camera, book of myths, schooner, ladder—which this speaker, entering her animal nature, can discard. As she does something natural, rather than unnatural, the sea shrinks to the intimacy of a pond in woods. Cold transforms itself magically to warmth. She who had to do everything "alone" in "Diving" is rewarded in her dream by a companion, "another animal / swimming under the snow-flecked surface of the pool." Moreover, where "Diving" closes under water, "Origins and History of Consciousness" resurfaces. It returns from dream to reality. The pond in woods becomes the city of muggers. But the poet recapitulates her decision of risked love as a descent "in a darkness / which I remember as drenched with light," and resolves to move outward. The poem ends with a sense of introducing Eros into Civilization.

"Natural Resources," another poem of transformations, revives and synthesizes two metaphors from *Snapshots:* the aerial cargo of the new woman, and the "abandoned mineshaft of doubt" in "Double Monologue." The latter poem had grieved that "our need mocks our gear." Now the mine is filled with certitude. A rainbow arches toward the core of a hill; the hill holds treasure yearning to be discovered. While "the routine of life" goes on above ground, the woman miner descends to hard labor in a kind of inverse astral projection. There she discerns images of the lives of past women, their precious domestic artifacts, the work they did and handed down from one generation to the next, the work that she must continue. Although "the women who first knew themselves / miners, are dead," the whole import of the poem is a celebration of a subterranean tradition of women's strength.

The technique employed in these two poems is a kind of overlay of transparencies. Present and past, reality and imagination, the life of the self and the lives of other selves, the spatially enclosed and the spatially unenclosed, are held in a tenuous, luminous balance. In the penultimate poem of *The Dream of a Common Language*, Rich depicts the synthesizing and liberating imagination in action. The place of "Toward the Solstice" is a country house, presumably the same one as in "From an Old House in America," and again there is feminine space: a room, the earth. Its time is "the thirtieth of November . . . the thirtieth of May," a first snowstorm and a spring torrent are falling outside, simultaneously, beautifully described in detail. The poet is "trying to hold in one steady glance / all the parts of my life," and is meditating on her need to perform a rite of separation between herself and the past. She realizes that the required ritual may be simply that she listen to her own pulse, which contains the falling snow and the rainstorm, and she both longs and fears to do this. The poem reminds me of Frost's "Directive" and of Blake's moment of "time less than a pulsation of the artery," which is equal to six thousand years because in this moment the poet's work is done. Rich is more tentative than either Blake or Frost. But she is being visionary. She is being metaphysical. The tyranny of Time, which is as real in our mental lives as any social or political tyranny, is mentally suspended here in a way I have not seen before. A philosophically developed feminism may mean an alternative idea of time and change, neither linear as in Hebrew tradition, cyclic as in classical philosophy, or juxtaposed against eternity as in Christianity. There is a flexing of the mind here, and no sense of an enemy. I am filled with curiosity to see more of what Rich can do along these lines, confident that whatever comes next will be an advance. What does not change is the pressure of Adrienne Rich's intelligence, as constant as the daylight in a love poem, "Nights and Days":

> I walk to an eastern window, pull up the blinds:
> the city around us is still

on a clear October morning
wrapped in her indestructible light.

NOTES

1. The figure in Arnold is impersonal and nonbiological; in Rich it is personal and biological. Rich's "you" is an unspecified woman who may be the poet or may be Everywoman. Although "The Mirror in Which Two are Seen As One" does not concern itself explicitly with collective as against individual experience, its implications (and this is typical for Rich) are social and historical. "The Mirror" appears in *Poems Selected and New, 1950–1974* (New York: W. W. Norton, 1974), p. 193.
2. "When We Dead Awaken" is in *On Lies, Secrets and Silence: Selected Prose 1966–1978* (New York: W. W. Norton, 1979).
3. "When We Dead Awaken," *On Lies, Secrets and Silence*, p. 45.
4. This is a central and well-argued idea in Dorothy Dinnerstein's recent *The Mermaid and the Minotaur* (New York: Harper and Row, 1977), a study of the effects on adult psychic and social life of the mother-infant bond, and the fact that there is no comparable father-infant bond. Dinnerstein feels that heterosexual romance is an attempt to re-create the emotional intensities of infancy.

A Wild Surmise

Motherhood and Poetry

That women should have babies rather than books is the con-
sidered opinion of Western civilization. That women should
have books rather than babies is a variation on that theme. Is it
possible, or desirable, for a woman to have both? What follows
here consists of some autobiographical remarks, offered on
the assumption that my history as a writer has something in
common with others of my generation; and a bit of exhortation
addressed to younger writers.

My initiation as a woman poet occurred when I was in my
first year of graduate school at the University of Wisconsin in
1960, writing poems as nearly resembling those of Keats,
Hopkins, and W. H. Auden as I could. We were visited that
year by a distinguished gentleman poet, to whom students
were invited to submit work for scrutiny and commentary. I
went for my conference hoping, of course, that he would tell
me I was the most brilliant young thing he had seen in twenty
years. Instead, he leafed through my slender sheaf and
stopped at a tame little poem in which, however, my husband
and I were lying in bed together, probably nude. "You women
poets are very graphic, aren't you," he said, with a slight shiver
of disgust.

Not having previously encountered this idea, I reacted in a
complex way. Certainly I was hurt and disappointed. At the
same time, something in me was drawing itself up, distending
its nostrils, thinking: "You're goddamned right, we are graph-
ic." I had not seen myself as a "we" until that moment. Like

Huck Finn deciding, "All right, then, I'll *go* to hell," I had just decided "All right, then, I'll *be* a woman poet," which meant I would write about the body.

A year out of graduate school, in 1965, I found myself in Cambridge, England, composing a poem about pregnancy and birth called "Once More Out of Darkness," later informally dubbed by my colleague Elaine Showalter, "A Poem in Nine Parts and a Post-Partum." The work was drawing from the experiences of two pregnancies, during which I had written numerous bits and scraps without intending anything so ambitious as a "long" poem, and it was thickening like soup. One morning when it was about two-thirds done, I realized that I had never in my life read a poem about pregnancy and birth. Why not? I had read hundreds of poems about love, hundreds of poems about death. These were, of course, universal themes. But wasn't birth universal? Wasn't pregnancy profound? During pregnancy, for example, I believed from time to time that I understood the continuity of life and death, that my body was a city and a landscape, and that I had personally discovered the moral equivalent of war. During the final stage of labor I felt like a hero, an Olympic athlete, a figure out of Pindar, at whom a stadium should be heaving garlands. At times, again, I was overwhelmed with loathing for the ugliness of my flesh, the obscenity of life itself, all this ooze, these fluids, the grossness of it. Trying to discover a poetic form which could express such opposite revelations simultaneously, and convey the extraordinary sensation of transformation from being a private individual self to being a portion of something else, I had the sense of being below the surface, where the islands are attached to each other. Other women knew what I knew. Of course they did, they always had. In that case, where were the poems?

At this time I had not read Sylvia Plath's "Three Women," a radio play consisting of three intertwined monologues in a maternity ward. Nor in fact had I heard of Plath. I had neither read nor heard of Rich's *Snapshots of a Daughter-in-Law* (1963), Sexton's *To Bedlam and Part Way Back* (1960) and *All My Pretty Ones* (1962), Diane Wakoski's *Inside the Blood Factory* (1962) or

Carolyn Kizer's "Pro Femina" (1963), in which the poet wise-cracks that women writers are "the custodians of the world's best-kept secret, / Merely the private lives of one-half of humanity." Though I had read *The Feminine Mystique*, I had not read Simone de Beauvoir. My field was nineteenth century, my dissertation on William Blake. Consequently I did not know that I had the good fortune to exist in a historical moment when certain women writers—mostly in utter isolation, unaware of each other's existence, twisted with shame, pain, fear of madness or the fact of it, and one of them already dead by her own hand—were for the first time writing directly and at large from female experience. The early grassblade slips through some crack in the dirt. It enters the cold alone, as Williams tells us in "Spring and All." It cannot guess how the ground will soon be covered with green fire. What I concluded, ignorant that this "we" existed, was that no poems had been written on the subject of pregnancy and childbirth, first because men could not write them. Love and death *sí*, pregnancy *no*. Second, women had not written the poems because we all reproduce the themes of previous poetry. One doesn't need a conspiracy theory here, just inertia. But third, pregnancy and birth were, I suddenly realized, subjects far more severely taboo than, for example, sex. One did not discuss pregnancy or birth in mixed groups. It was embarrassing. Threatening. Taboo because men were jealous of us, did not know they were, and we had to protect them from the knowledge. Threatening because we have a society which in many ways adores death and considers life disgusting. (In the same year that I wrote this poem, Lyndon B. Johnson was sworn in as President of the United States, having campaigned as the peace candidate committed to ending our involvement in Vietnam, against Barry Goldwater, who wanted to bomb North Vietnam back into the Stone Age.)

"Once More Out of Darkness" was published in 1970, and has since generated other poems. On one occasion when I read it to a graduate class in Women and Literature at Rutgers, arguing that writing and motherhood were not necessarily mutually exclusive enterprises, someone remarked that it was one thing to write about pregnancy, where you could be symbolic and spiritual, but quite impossible to use the squalling brats as poetic material after you had them, messing around underfoot, killing your schedule. This seemed a gauntlet flung down, which I had to seize in order to defend my opinion that you can write poetry about anything; that night I wrote "Babyshit Serenade," a poem in which I complain among other things that men don't do diapers, one happy result of which was that a man I know wrote a fine and funny poem called "Finding the Masculine Principle in Babyshit."

On another occasion, a group of students who had absorbed a certain line of militant feminist doctrine popular at the time greeted "Once More Out of Darkness" with an overt hostility I had not met before (male audiences and readers when hostile to women's writing either feign indifference or ladle condescension onto you—my dear, what a wonderful natural poem you've written, they say, meaning they think it required no intelligence or craftsmanship). My suggestion to this group that motherhood for me was like sex, a peck of trouble but I wouldn't want to go through life without it, was intended to produce laughter and illumination. Instead it produced outrage—motherhood to them was a burden imposed on women by patriarchy—which I took personally and defensively. The poem I wrote in what must be called rebuttal is titled "Propaganda." All these poems, I might mention, are formally experimental: a result of emotional involvement combined with intellectual tension, and a feeling of stumbling from shadow into hot sunlight. Often my poems on mothering and children come from more normal, less intense states, and are more conventional poetically; for example, "The Wolves," in my first book, which I think is a nice thing but not a discovery.

I began my most recent work on motherhood, *The Mother/Child Papers,* in 1970, when my third child and only son was born just after we invaded Cambodia and shot the four students at Kent State University. It was impossible at that time to avoid meditating on the meaning of having a boy child in time of war, or to avoid knowing that "time of war" means all of human history. Adrienne Rich in *Of Woman Born* quotes a

Frenchwoman declaring to her, when her son was born, "Madame, vous travaillez pour l'armée." Lady, you're working for the army. I had the despairing sense that this baby was born to be among the killed, or among the killers. What was I going to do about that, I who had been a pacifist since childhood, was then, and is now, a question. *The Mother/Child Papers* is, again, an experimental work for me, in the sense of posing formal problems correlative to moral ones. It begins with a section of prose about the Cambodian invasion paralleled with the delivery of my son in a situation of normal, that is to say exploitative, American medicine. A second section is a sequence of poems alternating between the consciousness of a mother and that of an infant, as the single fabric they are made of wears away and divides in two. Here a good deal of the excitement and difficulty lay in the attempt to imagine the changes in a newborn mind and invent a music for them. A third section consists of individual poems and prose-poems composed over the last ten years: a few scraps salvaged from the gullet of devouring Time, an enemy familiar to all mothers.

This brings me to the question raised by the activist and writer Alta, when she calls her book *Momma* "a start on all the untold stories." For women as artists, the most obvious truth is that the decision to have children is irrevocable. Having made it you are stuck with it forever; existence is never the same afterward, when you have put yourself, as de Beauvoir correctly says, in the service of the species. You no longer belong to yourself. Your time, energy, body, spirit and freedom are drained. You do not, however, lack what W. B. Yeats prayed for: an interesting life. In practical terms, you may ask yourself, "How can I ever write when I am involved with this *child*?" This is a real and desperate question. But can you imagine Petrarch, Dante, Keats, bemoaning their lot—"God, I'm so involved with this *woman*, how can I write?"

The advantage of motherhood for a woman artist is that it puts her in immediate and inescapable contact with the sources of life, death, beauty, growth, corruption. If she is a theoretician it teaches her things she could not learn otherwise; if she is a moralist it engages her in serious and useful work; if she is a romantic it constitutes an adventure which cannot be duplicated by any other, and which is guaranteed to supply her with experiences of utter joy and utter misery; if she is a classicist it will nicely illustrate the vanity of human wishes. If the woman artist has been trained to believe that the activities of motherhood are trivial, tangential to main issues of life, irrelevant to the great themes of literature, she should untrain herself. The training is misogynist, it protects and perpetuates systems of thought and feeling which prefer violence and death to love and birth, and it is a lie.

As writers like Rich, Dorothy Dinnerstein, Tillie Olsen, Phyllis Chesler, and Nancy Chodorow already demonstrate, it would be difficult to locate a subject at once more unexplored and more rich in social and political implication. Among the poets who have begun the exploration I would cite Plath, Sexton, Alta, Susan Griffin, Maxine Kumin, Lucille Clifton, Gwendolyn Brooks, Robin Morgan, Lisel Mueller, Sharon Olds, Patricia Dienstfrey, Alice Mattison, Marilyn Krysl—a beginning, a scratching of our surface.

The writer who is a mother should, I think, record everything she can: make notes, keep journals, take photographs, use a tape recorder, and remind herself that there is a subject of incalculably vast significance to humanity, about which virtually nothing is known because writers have not been mothers. "We think back through our mothers, if we are women," declares Woolf, but through whom can those who are themselves mothers, when they want to know what this endeavor in their lives means, do their thinking? We should all be looking at each other with a wild surmise, it seems to me, because we all need data, we need information, not only of the sort provided by doctors, psychologists, sociologists examining a phenomenon from the outside, but the sort provided by poets, novelists, artists, from within. As our knowledge begins to accumulate, we can imagine what it would signify to all women, and men, to live in a culture where childbirth and mothering occupied the kind of position that sex and romantic love have occupied in literature and art for the last five hundred years, or the kind of position that warfare has occupied since literature began.

I Make My Psyche from My Need

Only by reading is a text known, only by
interpretation is it entered. By reading
I mean an act of reading myself in the text,
understanding my hairs, my seeds, my rushing
waters, my journey . . . I make my Psyche
from my need. And when others need a
different Psyche, let them make it.
                    —Rachel DuPlessis, "Psyche, or Wholeness"

I.

When a woman rewrites an ancient myth it is not because she
yearns for a heroic past (when men were men, etc.). She is not
Ezra Pound, and she probably knows that she is happier in the
twentieth century than she would have been between the ages
of Homer and Pericles, locked in the *gynaeceum*. In all likeli-
hood she has two motives in mind, and the enjoyment of writ-
ing mythological poems has to do with the fact that the two
motives normally oppose each other.

One is her intent to be taken seriously as a writer. It happens
that to deal with ancient myth is to assume intellectual authori-
ty. She knows that much from her teachers.

The other is that she wants to get at something very deep in
herself, some set of feelings so intimate and strong that she is
ashamed.

The mythological poems many women are writing derive from a flash of connection. That story, that figure, that pattern of action—*I am the woman, I suffered, I was there. I* understand what Euridice felt. I see why the bacchantes tore apart the beautiful body of Orpheus, bloodying their hands and breasts.

> Ay me, I fondly dream!
> Had ye been there, for what could that have done?
> What could the Muse herself that Orpheus bore,
> The Muse herself for her enchanting son,
> When by the rout that made the hideous roar,
> His gory visage down the stream was sent,
> Down the swift Hebrus to the Lesbian shore?

John Milton wrote that because a poet acquaintance of his had recently drowned and he was about to embark on an ocean voyage himself. He thought he was too young to die, but the Fates might think otherwise, even though he planned to be a serious, a moral, a great poet, not some shoddy sonneteer sporting with Amaryllis in the shade.

> Fame is the spur that the clear spirit doth raise
> (That last infirmity of noble minds)
> To shun delights and live laborious days;
> But the fair guerdon when we hope to find,
> And think to burst out into sudden blaze,
> Comes the blind Fury with th'abhorred shears
> And slits the thin-spun life.

Even Orpheus, even Orpheus had not been safe, although his lyre had been given to him by Apollo himself, though a muse had been his mother and the charm of his music had quieted wild animals.

We cannot count the poets who have discovered themselves in Orpheus, Orpheus in themselves. We learn in school that all lyric poetry is at root Orphic, as Rilke too says. Here, however, in a poem by Sandra Gilbert called "Bas Relief: Bacchante," is one of those who made the hideous roar:

She's not at all as we expected, wearing
(instead of oiled breasts, a torn toga, a sexy swoon)
a sort of ruff and the calm look
of those animal-headed judges, wise as roots,
who rule the world below.

They were the ones, she says, who watched when Orpheus,
that show-off, gave the look that kills
to Euridice on the stony path.
Betrayed girl-bride, stuck halfway up the hill
and halfway down!
           Her fur ruff twitches
as she makes this case. It's clear
she never liked the bastard anyway,
the swaggering bastard with his silver flute,
precious proboscis, mean baton,

commanding silence, silence from everyone,
shutting the trees up, quieting the wind
and the quick birds, and the women.
Without his manly anthems
everything, she says, would sing, would sing.

I suppose the poet wrote that because she was angry. Orpheus,
or his sons, or his sons' sons, had angered her with all their
beauty. I suppose the poet would not write a poem about her
own personal impulse to tear some man apart.

II.

"I began reading these stories—of Pandora, Medea, Leda,
Helen, Prometheus, Orpheus, Jason—when I was six or seven
years old, and I remember still my sense of them as vivid but
mysterious, illustrations of something, I didn't know what, but
something very important," writes Gilbert.[1] We notice that
whenever we talk about these things we are assuming they are
not only true but important.

    In addition to literary ambition and the need to say some-
thing intimate about herself which she reads in the myth, the
woman poet may have a third motive. She intends to release an

imprisoned meaning. The poem is a great key she is jangling. She will fling the door open. Something will rush from the cell, feeling daylight on its face for the first time in centuries. "Not at all what we expected," notes Gilbert in "Bas Relief: Bacchante." "I see it now: this is / how it happened," she says at the opening of another poem called "Daphne." To "see" what was present but unseen by others. This last idea is crucial. It defines my sensation, when writing poems involving myths, that I am not inventing or "interpreting" but discovering.

In school I wrote a series of "Cassandra" poems, of which the male parent was Aeschylus' *Agammemnon*, where Cassandra has a magnificent mad-prophecy scene just before her death, stealing the show. The female parent was Louise Bogan's "Cassandra":

> To me one silly task is like another,
> I bare the shambling tricks of lust and pride.
> This flesh will never give a child its mother,—
> Song, like a wing, tears through my breast, my side,
> And madness chooses out my voice again,
> Again . . .

I loved both the haughtiness of that and its tormentedness. In my version Cassandra is a girl in love with Apollo. When he answers her maiden's prayer, she does put on his knowledge with his power—foreseeing not only the Trojan war but the utter indifference of the gods to human suffering. Refusing to bear Apollo's child because she wishes to create no new "flesh for the manglers in their mirth to rend," she is cursed with prophecy, becomes an embarrassment to her royal household with her crazy pacifism during the war with Greece, and in the final poem is mourning the death of Hector and wishing she could go truly crazy and forget her knowledge. What I remember about composing these poems is my conviction that I was telling what actually occurred, the way it must have been, what Homer and Aeschylus left out, even though I knew perfectly well that I was writing about myself: an arrogant, intellectual college girl, an outsider who often sat home Saturday nights, who remembered crying when other children stepped on ants and she could not stop them, who used to be teased, and who often wanted to scream, to scream at people. There was no contradiction, and it certainly did not matter that Cassandra belonged to a story. When did I ever think "history" was more true than "story"? Cassandra was real as I was, and my Cassandra was the real one.

Aristotle and his logician heirs tell you that nothing can be true and untrue at the same time. Such is the foundation of all rationality. One of the many pleasant results of experiencing a myth for yourself is that it shows you where Aristotle is wrong.

It is wonderful, in fact, how the imagination can see many contradictory things simultaneously. A poem in the *Mother/Child Papers* describes one of the few occasions in my life when I have experienced what Blake called "Double vision": that is, two images occupying the same visual field, one of them material, one spiritual. In this case the two objects were, first, my baby son who was kicking his legs while I diapered him, and second, a being of overwhelming energy and splendor who was emanating swiftly toward me from a radiating source that seemed to be in another dimension, whose infant form I recognized (Plato would say "remembered") immediately. *So that's where they come from,* was the flash. By "they" I meant the baby Eros with his arrows, the baby Hercules who kills the snake, the infant Jesus, the infant Krishna, and the child Blake saw on the cloud who commanded him to sing, all of whom lay there before my eyes. I have seldom been so privileged.

To enter or be entered by a myth makes plural vision possible, even necessary. Three days before I wrote the poem called "Homecoming" my house had been broken into while my husband was away at a conference, and I had been raped. The poem was written because I knew Penelope had in fact been raped by her suitors in Ithaca and that the story in Homer was a cover-up. I also knew that the *Odyssey* was written by a woman. Such revelations in no way interfere with equal and other findings. My friend Kate Ellis has a Penelope poem in which Troy is Vietnam and the suitors are draft-dodgers whom she shelters. I feel the same *yes, of course* response to this as I do to my own discovery that they were rapists. It is good that I can hold the different images together in my mind. They are rapists, they are friends, and so much else.

III.

It has something to do with pressure. Like water pressure. A hydraulic theory of creativity. One is a dam (grand-dam? Grendel's dam?) and one bursts. This is what I think when I begin a poem I have decided to call "Message from the Sleeper at Hell's Mouth." By the time I finish it I am less certain.

IV.

The book is called *Amor and Psyche* and is subtitled "The Psychic Development of the Feminine: A Commentary on the Tale by Apuleius by Erich Neumann." Neumann is the famous Jungian scholar, expert on archetypes, author also of *The Great Mother*. The version of the story that used to stand on my older daughter's bookshelf and now stands on my young son's, next to Madeleine L'Engle and C. S. Lewis' Narnia books, has a robin's egg blue cover and is called *Cupid and Psyche*. "Cupid," I check and see, is also his name in my tattered quarter-century-old copy of Apuleius' *Golden Ass*. His true name, though, is neither Amor nor Cupid. I know that much. His name is Eros. I check inside Neumann. Yes, Neumann too says Eros, explaining that his interest is in "the mighty god" of the myth, not the "frivolous" and "cunning" cherub. He knows that much. In fact, we all know enough to mistrust Apuleius' Roman urbanity. He tells his naive Greek folktale to a sophisticated audience for whom brilliance of prose is essential and the attitude toward sex must be social and worldly—but where did Apuleius get his tale? How old was it and what did it mean to him? How do we sense, reading Apuleius, that the sophistication is a trick, and that the author means us to read through the charming frivolity of his presentation, as if it were a backlit scrim, to the sweetness of the story? The effect is almost as if we were to see a Noel Coward play and feel, within or behind it, *The Tempest.* Or is this only hindsight, since at the end of *The Golden Ass* Apuleius dedicates himself—or his hero—to the priesthood of the Great Goddess at Eleusis? It would not have escaped his awareness that the goddess Demeter and her daughter Kore, who became Persephone, inhabit the same mythic world as Psyche.

These books are in my hand because I have received an essay from Rachel DuPlessis entitled "Psyche, or Wholeness."[2] Its opening sentence reads: "I want to write about Psyche, or Wholeness, but I am afraid, and this despite dreaming the moment of sitting down and writing psyche, wholeness, on the page." I recognize the pressure she speaks of. It happens I too have intended, for years, to write about Psyche, and this essay, I think, will be the final weight that moves me. Her second paragraph begins:

> But this great scholar is wrong. Neumann—wrong. When I say this, I see my father, deep walnut bookshelves filled with books; no, I refuse to see him, but I do, and I know and do not admit the whole of what I am seeing. I say: I needed this, you needed that. I say: I do not believe your interpretation. But he has studied! And I have not. Yet I know what I want to feel, and I want to make the myth tell me that.

So do I. It is difficult for DuPlessis to write. The thought of the journey is interrupted by a memory of her father at his desk, her mother typing the manuscripts of her father, herself unable to learn the Greek alphabet he has given her to learn. One father glides into another father, and there is Neumann, who has led her to penetrate the Psyche story, has drawn her in and in. Neumann has revealed to her the heroic female who is not like a male because she does not aggressively slay dragons, and not like a typical female because she is not passive but active. He has defined true femininity as adventure, *gnosis*, rule-breaking, change. Then Neumann has betrayed her.

For years I have meant to write about Psyche. Since I read

Apuleius in school? Since in my twenties I realized for the first time how I loved my girlfriend Annie? Since the first time I kissed a man through and through?

Psyche is a girl so beautiful men worship her, forsaking the temples of Aphrodite. The goddess orders her son Eros to punish this upstart, but instead he secretly falls in love with her. An oracle commands that on her wedding day Psyche must be dressed as for a funeral and abandoned at a cliff's edge. When this is done she is wafted to a palace in a hidden valley, where her every need is attended to by invisible servants, and her mysterious husband visits her nocturnally and departs by daybreak. Psyche is happy, but when her sisters visit they tell her she has wed a monstrous serpent who will soon devour her; she must light a lamp when he falls asleep and prepare to kill him. Following this advice, Psyche discovers that her husband is the lovely God of Love himself. But oil from the lamp burns his arm and wakes him. Angry, he flies away from the palace, leaving Psyche deserted. That is the first part of the story. When you hear it you feel you have always known it. So many folktales are like this, there is a sense of necessity in the pattern.

In the second part of the story Psyche seeks for Eros and is made to perform impossible tasks by Aphrodite. She is helped in each task by natural creatures—ants, a reed, an eagle. (Because she is beautiful? Because she is innocent? What is the relation of Psyche to nature?) This part of the story is like a female version of the labors of Hercules. In the end she is supposed to fetch from Hades a box of Persephone's beauty—but she opens it and is put to sleep by the miasma within. Now Eros, healed of his wound and his anger, flies to her and frees her, and the gods agree that she shall wed Eros in heaven and be granted immortality.

Why does the story make me so glad?

The first person I knew who was Psyche was my friend Annie Heyward who lived on the fifth floor of my building in the Project. There were eight children in that family. The mother and father drank, and if I am reconstructing the costumes and makeup of the two older sisters correctly they must have turned tricks downtown. Annie did the family laundry and ironing, and minded the babies. Twice Annie ran away from home to live with an aunt, twice she was sent home. Yet all I remember of her is merriment and laughter, blue Irish eyes, blonde Irish curls that bounced about her shoulders. So pretty. So warm. Annie on the seesaw flying into the air when I hit bottom, Annie defending me when other children wanted to hit me, Annie dealing cards. In the locker room of the pool, a naked being with actual breasts and a triangle of glinting hair, amid smells of chlorine and urine, laughing at her own jokes.

When Annie and her boyfriend kissed, romantically, I saw a blossoming tree, fuller than the plane trees in the Project ever were. I was supposed to be kissing Annie's brother, but it wasn't the same thing, I knew that much. The four of us were in the elevator going up and down, pressing Five, pressing One. In between kisses she giggled.

After her father killed himself she said to me, "Do you know why I'm sorry my father died? Who'll walk down the aisle with me when I get married?" Then I was ashamed of her, later of myself. It would please me to think that Annie never to this day has embraced a man without pleasure, but the odds are very poor, are they not? What might the odds be that her innocence has escaped rape, beatings, welfare, the bottle, drugs? What good can it do her that in my twenties I found, under my jealousy, a clear pool of love for her? I moved away when she was fourteen and I was twelve, because I got a scholarship somewhere, and I did not see her again. There was a girl in college who was also blonde, rosy, beautiful as an armful of peonies, and so nice that nobody could hate her. There was Marilyn Monroe, laughing and bouncing, an inspired comedienne whose fate we know.

"I don't look at myself as a commodity, but I'm sure a lot of people have," says Marilyn in a *Life* magazine interview printed the week of her death.

In the story she wins. She is not crushed in the story. She succeeds, her laughter prevails, her innocence prevails, her sexuality prevails. So she comes to her lover, he to her, there and only there.

My first Eros was an Italian boy with large brown eyes and softness about him. Candy in his pockets. I trailed his heels like a kitten before kindergarten. Another time there was my husband walking or floating naked from a forest's edge, his dark brown curls glossy and wild, his lips open, thigh muscles firm, or rather an image of him. An older image of my father doing push-ups. One knew by now that no man was the same as the wild god, of whom one dreamed or daydreamed, imagining his sandaled feet on the stone, and that if the god ever materialized one would follow him gladly.

In Bombay I saw him actually playing his flute in the garden under the palace balcony; sitting on a tree limb smiling at the *gopis* in the pond whose clothing he had mischievously stolen—they have to come out of the water or he won't give their clothes back—solemnly embracing *Radha* while attendants looked on, a necklace of white jasmine against his blue skin and silken robes. It is true that you can fall in love with a picture and there were so many pictures in the exhibition. It is true that I was breathing strangely even when I went down the marble steps. For days, trying to be a tourist, I was beside myself, until I bought a fat volume of *Kangra Paintings on Love* to alleviate my condition. Like hot metal plunged in water, then, I hissed and cooled.

I am so happy Psyche has Eros in the story. In this way I have him too. We are not destroyed. We succeed.

When I began to write "Message from the Sleeper at Hell's Mouth," I thought the wisest policy would be to avoid rereading Apuleius. It went well so long as I worked on the supporting characters. The poet, in love with her heroine, aware that love is a delusion and the heroine is destroyed in practice, saying here for once it will be different. The mother surrendering the innocent daughter to a wedding, that is, to destruction. Why does she do it? The sisters—how does it feel, my dears, to have the most beautiful girl on earth, worshipped by mankind, as your sister? Awful, no? Small wonder you behave badly. I discovered, when I could not make the sisters speak in chorus, that there must really have been two of them with different characters, one of them jealous and spiteful, the other one worshipful and clinging. And Aphrodite, the cruel goddess, proud and passionate, whose only child is Love, and she cannot keep him.

These are persona poems. It is understood that all the characters are aspects of myself. When I come to Psyche I see "clearly and distinctly" (cf. Descartes, *Discourse on Method*) something others fail to see. That she is beautiful, innocent and good—everyone knows. Psyche is the Soul. Yet they laugh at her in a way. They equate "innocence" with "ignorance." They think, because she seems to do what she is told, she is a dizzy blonde. A "dumb bunny," as Sexton calls Snow White. They do not credit her with wisdom. No. My Psyche is confidence, certainty, emotional ease and openness; she is also knowledge, of a mysterious and yet absolute kind.

To adventure is to learn—she sees who her husband is, her sisters, the goddess, the tasks too are philosophical—but in some way she knows it all from the beginning, the way we can know a melody but not remember it until we sing the first phrase, then the next comes, and so on.

> Whatever happened, I said
> yes, and discovered that every
> time I said it I could
> see further, more completely.

I say she says that. Psyche is my awareness that I am good and cannot fail. Psyche is my capacity to kiss a lover through and through. When an event approaches me and I do not shrink, there is my Psyche. Without this certainty, even if there is just a drop of it, surrounded everywhere by poisonous doubt and perplexity, there can be no Psyche. And if this certainty is clear in the beginning, and grows clearer—?

The part about the box of beauty Psyche fetches from Hades is a conundrum. She must not open it but she does and it puts her to sleep. Neumann says, "Psyche fails, she must fail, because she is a feminine Psyche. . . . By preferring beauty to knowledge, she reunites herself with the feminine in her nature . . . she does this lovingly and for Eros."

Like DuPlessis when she comes to this point in Neumann, I stop cold here, angry. That femininity equals failure cannot be the meaning, it must be a betrayal and a stupidity. There was no beauty in the box. It was sleep. The knockout drops. The cosmetic ads. As the hero must descend to Hades, dying symbolically in order to rise, the wearied heroine must on her hell-trip die this particular death of wanting applied beauty, somebody else's beauty, beauty-in-a-box. What the box contains is not-self, an alluring solipsistic lie, a way to stop instead of move. She must try it to learn what it means.

Apuleius says:

> There was no beauty therein, nor anything save a hellish and truly Stygian sleep, which, so soon as it was set free by the removal of the lid, rushed upon her and poured over all her limbs in a thick cloud of slumber. She fell in the very path where she stood, and the sleep possessed her where she fell.

Apuleius says, when the god descended to rescue her, "he wiped the sleep from off her and confined it in the casket, its former receptacle." Then Psyche can wake, rise, move. Imagine a Psyche who will never again touch Touch-and-Glo or Revlon.

But in that sleep of death what dreams may come? When we sleep we dream, we dream one truth or another, and Psyche must certainly dream because one sort of knowledge remains closed to her despite her adventures. Having comprehended the world, nature, society, she has not seen herself. So at the moment she becomes who she is not—a woman in a coma, a woman covered with cosmetics—is it possible she sees what she is? She is the Soul, crawling, let us say, up a wire fence—her wings out of the cocoon—and I see her seeing it. When Eros comes to save her, she is already saved.

Yet I do not write the poem. There is a part I cannot write. It hurts me. I put it off. Six months, eight months.

I went back to Apuleius. It was true, what I feared, and not an authorial flourish, but a very basic root of the story. When Eros first abandons her, Psyche goes directly to one sister, then the other. She tells them each in turn that they have been chosen as Eros' new brides, and are to leap from the crag where Psyche originally married. When they leap, of course, they are dismembered on the rocks. Much later, prepared to undertake the journey to Hell, Psyche is warned to give no pity to the dead who will importune her from Styx's waters, and she obeys this instruction.

Intolerable. My Psyche, this has been so important to me for so many years of childhood, student life, marriage, three children, friends, lovers, students of my own, no matter how I stray, my Psyche is kindness itself. Never, never willingly would she do harm. She would never refuse pity to the pitiable. Impossible for revenge to coexist with her openness, or for her to say no instead of yes. She might as well, in that case, be Caesar or Stalin. She might as well have been manning the ovens, or be a cop shooting down a black kid in Los Angeles, they all have their filthy reasons, excuses, political imperatives, she might as well be in a corporate think tank discussing *triage*, as be my Psyche.

We gathered here today knew only Marilyn—a warm human being, impulsive and shy, sensitive and in fear of rejection, yet ever avid for life and reaching out for fulfillment.
　　　　　　　　　—Lee Strasberg, August 8, 1962

She was pure of heart. She was free of guile . . . There is not the slightest evidence that she ever experienced envy or jealousy; cruelty would have been completely outside her range even if she could have brought herself to desire it.
—Edward Wagenknecht, *Marilyn Monroe, A Composite Biography*

But I want to finish the poem. To finish the poem I must let the sisters die. No, I must kill them. Amazing how difficult this is, to see that my sisters will die, blocked, futureless, and that the dead are dead forever.

No. Yes. A contradiction. The three books, the essay, the drafts of the poem on my desk, the desire to go forward, the pressure to stay back. Do I remember what I said about Aristotle being wrong because in the imagination contradictions can coexist, and myths exist to teach us that? No within yes, then, the power of evil within the power of good in my Psyche. I must put it there myself, without knowing if it is like a stone inside a loaf of bread, or like a seed inside of fruit. Killing and coldness, deep inside the story, so that I can fall asleep, dream myself out of the cocoon with my white wings pursuing my wounded beloved, can finish the poem.

Do I remember thinking the myth-poem is written when something lies so deep we are ashamed, and am I certain what shames me?

Does Annie, anyway, want this poem?

> . . . *the swarming dead implored me for a single*
> *touch, a single kiss.*
> *No, I said.*

The poem is completed, was able to come around after I wrote that. I have made it as light as possible, not clogged with cogitations. Still I am in the middle of my journey. Whether my Psyche is completed I don't know.

NOTES

1. Sandra Gilbert's talk, "Confessional Mythology," was given at a Modern Language Association Seminar on Women and Mythology in 1980. Her poems "Bas Relief: Bacchante" and "Daphne" appeared in *Massachusetts Review* (Winter 1976) and *Poetry Northwest* (Summer 1977).
2. Rachel DuPlessis' essay "Psyche, or Wholeness," appears in *Massachusetts Review* (Spring 1979):77–96.

Afterword

To say "poetess" is and always has been a gentle insult. A poetess is a poet who is sensitive and knows how to feel, perhaps very intensely, but does not know how to think or judge. She has no authority to change our minds. She asks us to bring her flowers and perfume to console her for her powerlessness and disguise it from her, lest she become sullen; we pretend to respect her. The term has gone out of favor, which in some ways is a pity. I suspect that many of the poetesses writing today are men.

To say "she writes like a man" used to be a compliment, but few women today would take it so. "She writes like a man" does not mean she writes with all her energies. It means she can think, organize, judge, even argue, but will not embarrass us with messy female emotions. Whoever "writes like a man" but *is* not a man is pretending not to have a body, or passions, unlike the men who write like men.

In the future our poetry, literature and art may become genderless. I do not mean sexless, or asexual: we have asexual poetry, or attempts at it, everywhere around us, and it is appealing in the same way that the idea of a sexless life is appealing. The fiery muck of our bodies, like oil spills burning, creates difficulty for us all and is unsightly and wasteful besides, so it is no wonder we want, the poet wants, to rise out of it into the celibacy of a plain brain, pure cognition. To my taste, when that wish is granted, the result is boring. Poetry that feels asexual to me is like the potato skins and carrot scrapings I was urged as a child to eat because they were "the best part." There is a sense of airy fetters. The poet is afraid of something, which is normal, and has surrendered to the fear—which is also normal, but does not produce great poetry. A poet's profile can be so low, so down around the ankles, that I cannot see it if I look upward or straight ahead. To eliminate sexuality in language is to eliminate vitality.

When I say "genderless," then, I mean not sexless but something like bisexual or androgynous or omnisexual, containing rather than excluding the two (or four or six) sexes latent in writers and readers. The greatest writers in the world are always approaching genderlessness, because there is no nook or cranny of their natures, their experiences, their dream lives, that does not get swept into their art. They do not arrive *at* genderlessness. Virginia Woolf, who said Shakespeare did, was thinking wishfully. Even Whitman, though he is "of the female as well as the male," is discernably closer to being a gent than a lady. For men and women in the world are socially assigned such very different degrees of power, such very different behavior, and artists must hold a mirror to the world as well as their own souls.

As for women writers, I believe the stronger and more free they are, the more they will, for the time being, write like women; and the more they write like women, the stronger they will become. If the process continues, and especially if life in this respect imitates art, we may one day, for the first time, know what it means to be a "woman," to be a "man," to be "human." By then of course the meanings will be different.

UNDER DISCUSSION
Donald Hall, General Editor

Volumes in the Under Discussion series collect reviews and essays about individual poets. The series is concerned with contemporary American and English poets about whom the consensus has not yet been formed and the final vote has not been taken. Titles in the series include:

Please write for further information on available editions and current prices.

Ann Arbor

The University of Michigan Press

Printed and bound by CPI Group (UK) Ltd, Croydon, CR0 4YY

09/06/2025

14685672-0001